PICTURE

TO THE

WILD FLOWERS

OF

NORTH EAST

YORKSHIRE

Nan Sykes

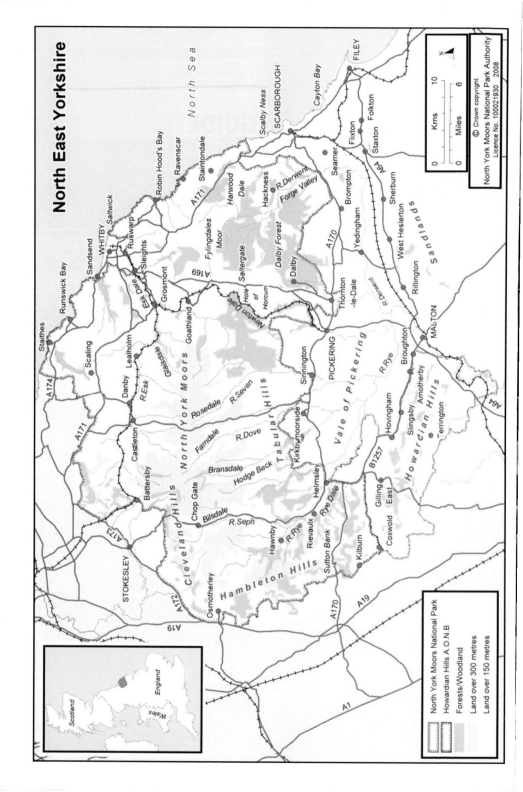

North East Yorkshire

CONTENTS

Published by the North York Moors National Park Authority 2008

© Copyright Nan Sykes 2008

ISBN 978-1-904622-20-8

[petals includes petal-like sepals]   **COLOUR KEY TO FLOWERS**

flower parts in 3 (or 6)	2 or 4 petals	5 or more similar petals		BELL, FUNNEL or TUBE
bog asphodel 173	cabbage 61	agrimony 85	mullein 131	barberry 102
daffodil 173	charlock 60	avens 86	musk 133	comfrey 122
mignonette 59	crosswort 142	buttercup 29-31	pansy 57	cow-wheat 132
winter	flixweed 63	celandine 32	primrose 73	cowslip 73
aconite 32	golden saxifrage 79	cinquefoil 88,89	silverweed 89	henbane 118
yellow iris 176	greater celandine 39	currant 76	spearwort 32	honeysuckle 143
yellow star-of-	lady's bedstraw 142	fiddleneck 120	St. John's-wort 54,55	yellow
Bethlehem 172	mustard 60,62	globe flower 31	stonecrop 77	bird's-nest 138
	moschatel 103	gromwell 119	tutsan 55	yellow corydalis 36
	rape 60	loosestrife 74	rock-rose 56	
	rocket 61	marsh marigold 31	yellow pimpernel 75	
	tormentil 88	monkey-flower 133	yellow-wort 116	
	wallflower 63			
	weld 59			
	Welsh poppy 39			
	winter-cress 62			
	yellow-cress 62			
garlic 175	bedstraw 141	bogbean 104	pearlwort 43	climbing
snowdrop 171	bittercress 65	black nightshade 118	raspberry 82	corydalis 36
ramsons 175	cleavers 141	bramble 82	rose 81	comfrey 122
snowflake 171	dittander 67	campion 42	sandwort 48	cowberry 71
water-plantain 177	dogwood 100	catchfly 42	saxifrage 78	fumitory 37
	dwarf cornel 100	chickweed 44	snow-in-summer 46	bindweed 117
	enchanter's	chickweed-	spurrey 47	lily-of-the-valley 172
	nightshade 100	wintergreen 73	stitchwort 45	milkwort 108
	hoary-cress 67	crane's-bill 108	stonecrop 77	snowdrop 171
	horse-radish 67	dewberry 82	strawberries 86	snowflake 171
	pennycress 63	dodder 117	sundew 72	solomon's seal 174
	pepperwort 67	dropwort 87	spring beauty 49	star-of-
	pigmyweed 77	fairy flax 104	wood anemone 35	Bethlehem 171
	privet 101	grass-of-Parnassus 78	wood-sorrel 104	wintergreen 69
	rock-cress 64	gromwell 119	water crowfoot 33	
	scurvygrass 68	mouse-ear 46	water-lily 177	
	sea mouse-ear 46	musk mallow 56	violet 58	
	shepherd's-purse 68			
	spindle 101			
	swine-cress 64			
	thale cress 64			
	traveller's joy 35			
	watercress 65			
	whitlowgrass 64			
	wild radish 60			
	woodruff 142			
butcher's	moschatel 103	bryony 59		
broom 174	spurge laurel 101	hellebore 34		

PEA and CLOVER	DAISY or BRUSH		LIPPED and ORCHIDS	UMBELS and SPIKES
bird's-foot trefoil 96 broom 95 dyer's-greenweed 95 gorse 95 kidney vetch 92 meadow vetchling 91 medick 94 melilot 93 petty whin 95 tree lupin 93 trefoil 94,96	carline thistle 149 cat's-ear 161 colt's-foot 164 corn marigold 164 dandelion 157 elecampane 161 fleabane 164 fox-and-cubs 158 goat's-beard 159 goldenrod 165 groundsel 163 gum plant 161 hawkbit 157 hawk's-beard 160	hawkweed 157-8 leopard's-bane 164 leptinella 155 lettuce 159 nipplewort 159 oxtongue 158 pineappleweed 163 ploughman's spikenard 165 ragwort 162 sow-thistle 156 tansy 165	bladderwort 139 bird's-nest orchid 170 fluellen 138 hemp-nettle 129 toadflax 138 wood sage 128 yellow archangel 129 yellow-rattle 132	alexanders 111 broomrape 139 cudweed 152 lady's bedstraw 142 lady's mantle 87 mugwort 151 pepper-saxifrage 113
bird's-foot 92 clover 97 wood vetch 91	daisy 152 dog daisy 152 feverfew 153 fleabane 155 mayweeds 153 shaggy soldier 153 sneezewort 154 yarrow 154		dead-nettle 124 eyebright 134 gypsywort 127 hemp-nettle 129 helleborine 169 orchid 168-170	angelica 111 baneberry 34 burnet-saxifrage 112 celery 114 chervil 109 cow parsley 109 dropwort 87 elder 143 fool's parsley 112 fool's watercress 115 ground elder 114 guelder rose 143 hedge parsley 110 hemlock 110 hogweeed 111 marshwort 115 may lily 174 meadow rue 35 meadowsweet 87 persicaria, pale 52 pignut 112 shepherd's needle 114 sweet cicely 110 water dropwort 114 water-parsnip 115 wild carrot 113 wood sanicle 113
			frog orchid 170 twayblace 170	

[petals includes petal-like sepals]

flower parts in 3 (or 6)	2 or 4 petals	5 or more similar petals		BELL, FUNNEL or TUBE
flowering rush 175 meadow saffron 174	coralroot 66 cranberry 71 cuckoo flower 66 dame's violet 66 gentian 116 honesty 66 madder 142 mezereon 101 rosebay 98 scurvygrass 68 sea rocket 68 speedwell 135 willowherb 98,99	bird's-eye primrose 73 bog pimpernel 75 fairy foxglove 134 campion 42 cornsalad 144 crane's-bill 106,107 centaury 116 dodder 117 gentian 116 herb-robert 108 mallow 56 pink 49	pink purslane 49 purple loosestrife 79 ragged-robin 43 rose 80,81 sea-milkwort 74 soapwort 43 spurrey 47 stork's-bill 108 valerian 144 water avens 86 water-violet 74	bell heather 70 bindweed 117 bog-rosemary 71 comfrey 122 cross-leaved heath 70 cowberry 71 foxglove 132 fumitory 37 heather 70 milkwort 108 snowberry 143 toothwort 139
	speedwell 135-7	Abraham, Isaac and Jacob 120 bittersweet 118 borage 120 bugloss 120 columbine 34 cornsalad 144 crane's-bill 106	forget-me-not 121 green alkanet 119 periwinkle 57 teaplant 118 Venus's looking-glass 140 violet 57,58	bellflower 140 bluebell 172 comfrey 122 harebell 140 milkwort 108 thorn-apple 118 viper's bugloss 119
	poppy 39	currants 76 marsh cinquefoil 09 scarlet pimpernel 75	red valerian 144	bilberry 71 deadly nightshade 118

Some plants cannot easily be identified from the above keys; their flowers may be very tiny, or grow without petals (goosefoot); or be concealed within the structure of the plant (wild arum); or grow in an irregular shape (fly and bee orchids, balsams); or have multi-coloured petals (knotgrass). See also:

arrowgrass 179
blinks 49
bog-myrtle 36
bulrush 178
cottongrass 69
crowberry 72
dock 50

duckweed 179
fat-hen 40
Good King Henry 40
Herb-Paris 173
ivy 105
mare's-tail 178
mercury 102

milfoil 178
mugwort 151
nettle 38
orache 41
parsley-piert 87
pellitory-of-the-wall 38
plantain 130

pondweed 179
sorrel 51
spurge 103
starwort 177
water-pepper 53
water-purslane 79

PEA and CLOVER	DAISY or BRUSH	LIPPED and ORCHIDS	UMBELS and SPIKES
bird's-foot 92 clover 96,97 restharrow 93 vetch 90,91	burdock 150 butterbur 146 fleabane 155 knapweed 147 mountain everlasting 146 sawwort 147 scabious 145 seaside daisy 155 teasel 145 thistles 148-150 winter heliotrope 146	bartsia 132 basil 126 betony 123 black horehound 128 calamint 126 dead-nettle 124 helleborine 169 lousewort 133 marjoram 128 mint 125 orchid 166-8 red hemp-nettle 129 thyme 126 toadflax 138 woundwort 123	angelica 111 bistort 52 bridewort 87 hedge parsley 110 hogweed 111 toothwort 139 hemp-agrimony 154
tare 92 vetch 90, 91	blue fleabane 155 blue sow-thistle 151 cornflower 151 sea aster 151	bugle 127 butterwort 139 basil thyme 126 ground-ivy 126 monk's-hood 35 selfheal 127 skullcap 128 wild clary 127	
	fox-and-cubs 158		redshank 52

INTRODUCTION

This book is a photographic record of wild flower and native tree species throughout North East Yorkshire (the area shown on the map on p.2), excluding ferns, most sedges, grasses and rushes, hybrids, sub-species and planted alien trees.

The purpose of the book is three-fold. One purpose is to facilitate identification of the c.700 wild flowers established in this area. By eliminating the remaining c.1400 species which occur in the rest of Britain, naming a plant is made easier and less prone to error.

A further purpose of the book is to define the local flora in the first decade of the C21st against which future changes may be assessed. Global warming is likely to affect the overall appearance of the countryside as well as drainage, flooding, food and bio-fuel production. Monitoring the status of wild flowers provides valuable data in relation to these matters.

A third purpose is to encourage a wider understanding of the vital role which plants play in sustaining all living creatures, including mankind. The countryside is highly valued as a recreational antidote to the pressures of today's urbanised life-style. But its importance in maintaining a reservoir of potential food plants and medicinal remedies is widely ignored. Unlike previous generations, few people now have close links with the land and its natural vegetation. Although only a fraction of plant species have been examined so far for their possible beneficial qualities, each year brings yet more extinctions, due in part to unawareness of either their presence or importance. It is essential to encourage a wider understanding of plants as the life-sustaining basis of our environment and their place in today's countryside. A good way to start is by looking for, enjoying and protecting, wild flowers around us.

Conservation organisations and voluntary societies strive to restore the former rich bio-diversity of our land, with varying degrees of success linked to inadequate funding. But alongside these formalised strategies stands a need for greater public involvement. Wild flowers cannot thrive in isolated protected pockets. We need to relax our obsession for tidyness, and allow millions of acres covered by road verges and open spaces, parts of our gardens and field edges to provide havens where wild flowers can flourish to form a sustainable network across the wider countryside. A viable self-supporting flora can support other wildlife and enhance the visual landscape without impacting on economic land use.

Plants are great opportunists; where one species fails another soon fills the space. We need to provide that space for without flowers and their seeds, we lose not only the insects, butterflies, mammals and birds which depend upon them but unknown future resources for mankind.

NORTH EAST YORKSHIRE

Although not an administrative region, North East Yorkshire is a unique ecological area within the county of North Yorkshire. It extends across the North York Moors National Park, the Howardian Hills of Outstanding Natural Beauty, and nearly 50 miles (80km) of Heritage Coast together with many botanically-rich sites in a variety of different habitats. Located on the eastern side and half-way between the north and south of Britain, it includes ancient woodland, forestry plantations, extensive heather moorland, hill and arable farmland, sea cliffs and shores, grassy dales and various wetlands, lakes, and river systems.

Across about 1320 sq miles (3418 sq km) of changing landscape, it stretches from the craggy edge of high moorland overlooking Tees-side in the north to the foothills of the Yorkshire Wolds skirting the Vale of Pickering in the south, approximately 30 miles (48km). From its western perimeter of steep escarpments on the Cleveland and Hambleton Hills above the Vales of Mowbray and York, it spreads 44 miles (70km) to the North Sea coast in the east. Altitude rises from sea-level to sea-cliffs at Boulby 613ft (186m) and moorland up to 1449ft (442m) near Urra.

North East Yorkshire has a small resident population, principally involved in farming and tourism, but attracts large numbers of summer visitors. Urban development is limited to major coastal resorts of Filey, Scarborough and Whitby, and market towns of Helmsley, Kirkbymoorside and Pickering, with numerous villages and hamlets.

Landscape

The soils and topography reflect the varied bedrocks which span the Jurassic sequence from acidic shales, sandstones, ironstones and grits to limestones and clays. [North-east Yorkshire coastal cliffs provide a rare exposure of the full Jurassic strata]. Superimposed is the legacy of glaciation. Overall the land tilts south-easterly with much of the northern part forming a near level plateau – the North York Moors – criss-crossed by river valleys, dales, steep gills and crags to provide endless variety of aspect, soils, gradient and temperature.

As the moorland plateau sinks steadily lower towards the south-east, it confronts an east to west series of nabs (protrusions of higher land). These form the northern exposure of a band of fertile corallian limestones up to 5miles (8km) north to south, and stretching some 30miles (48km) from Murton and Sutton Bank in the west to Silpho and Suffield in the east. This limestone belt continues the southerly tilt until it is overlain by alluvium deposited in the former Lake Pickering – now mostly flat, fertile arable land.

Before extensive drainage schemes, from the C18th onwards, transformed this meltwater lake and marsh into farmland, its waters lapped sandy shores – today evident in sandy fields along its southern edge and in numerous working or abandoned sand and gravel quarries.

Towards the south-west lies a different terrain midway in character between the rugged uplands and surrounding flat plains. Designated as the Howardian Hills Area of Outstanding Natural Beauty, it features leisurely streams meandering amongst gently undulating hills, and wet woodlands in secluded valleys. It covers about 80 sq miles (207 sq km) with small villages spread amongst extensive parkland, farms and plantations, and fragments of dry heath on sandy moraines.

Arrival of Plants

Until about 12,000 years ago most of northern Britain was covered by deep ice and snow, inhibiting all but the hardiest tundra-type vegetation. North East Yorkshire lay at the southern fringe of an extended arctic. It was gripped by two vast glaciers, one moving down from Scandinavia in the east, the other thrusting in from the Vale of Mowbray to the west. Isolated above the ice sheets lay what is today's moorland plateau, then a permafrosted wilderness. Increasing temperatures led to meltdown and the formation of Lake Eskdale and Lake Pickering with countless smaller lakes, swamps and swollen waterways. Retreating glaciers left sand and gravel moraines, hanging valleys and land-locked bogs or swangs. Rising water levels cut new channels such as Newtondale, and moraine dams diverted water courses including the River Derwent. Immense deposits of glacial till or boulder clay (a random mass of material transported by glaciers) spread deeply, especially along the coast.

Eventually water levels started to subside, exposing new habitat into which plants and animals could migrate northwards from non-glaciated terrain. Ameliorating climate encouraged the establishment of wildwood, a mosaic of changing tree species, ground flora, wetland and glades.

From about 5,000 years ago, humans – first as nomadic hunters then as settlers – increasingly influenced wildlife. Natural forest cover was reduced to provide better hunting, grazing and crop-growing land. Soil nutrients were soon exhausted on exposed upland, leading to peat accumulation and the spread of heather and other acid-tolerant species. Impenetrable swamps were drained and suitable land brought under cultivation as human settlements and farming increased. Vegetative cover changed according to land-use; new species were introduced both by man and natural causes.

With small interference from a low-density population and open-field farming, a diverse flora developed. Owing to the location of North East Yorkshire, fringing both northern uplands and southern lowlands, species variety was enhanced by several plants at the limits of their geographical range. (see appendix A). Local floras, compiled from 1888 onwards, indicate earlier abundant variety, distribution and quantity of plants, including many no longer seen in this area.

Changing Flora

Perhaps the first major impact on wildflowers came with land enclosure into private ownership and innovative management from the C18th onwards, although sufficient lightly-managed land remained for most species to survive. But serious problems for much wildlife developed in the C20th. A threat to the nation's food and timber supplies in the aftermath of two world wars heralded maximum land conversion to intensify food production and create a softwood national forest.

Now termed 'The C20th Agricultural Revolution', a rapid transformation of the countryside was facilitated by advancing technology which enabled new farming methods, crops, means of weed and pest control. Throughout the land natural vegetation was annihilated in favour of intensive food and timber cropping.

It is likely that the 1970s were the nadir for wild flowers. By the 1980s the spectre of a land bereft of wildlife raised alarm in many circles and provoked a national policy to restore plant biodiversity – a much more challenging task than its desecration a few decades earlier.

One problem is that surviving flower-rich pockets are now so widely dispersed that cross-pollination is often impossible, causing populations to die out rather than spread. North East Yorkshire today is home to nearly 700 wild flower species, (approximately a third of the total British flora), but more than 100 of these survive in dangerously small populations with several reduced to a few plants on solitary sites. Two species – red hemp-nettle and burnt orchid – are listed nationally as on the brink of extinction. At least 40 species are known to have become extinct locally in the past 100 years. *(see Appendix B)*.

Another challenge in the struggle to rescue the former rich diversity is the effect of global warming. Already noticeable is later autumn leaf-fall, and unusual flowering times are evident during milder winters and warmer summers. As butterfly, insect and bird populations re-locate in response to changing climate, pollination and seed dispersal of plants will be affected and need to adjust. Some plants will re-locate to more congenial sites in tune with temperature range and rainfall distribution. Although wildlife has always responded to changing weather patterns, it may now have to adapt at an unprecedented rate; some species will succeed – others may face extinction. Many will need selective re-introduction; all will need sympathetically-managed land, gardens and road verges throughout the countryside if they are to survive. The only certainty is that change is underway.

12

ACKNOWLEDGEMENTS

This book could not have been compiled without help from many colleagues. Requests to search for species, identify specimens, study personal records and solve botanical dilemmas have met with generous co-operation, accompanied by a few surprises and problems, together with much enthusiastic shared-studying of North East Yorkshire's wild flowers.

Gill Smith (Botanical Recorder for Ryedale Natural History Society) has located unusual species and habitats in lesser-known parts of the Howardian Hills, advised on species identification, solved computer problems and searched the pages for botanical errors. Margaret Atherden has explored with me every road verge in North East Yorkshire; tramped along rail ballast and track-sides from Whitby to Battersby and Pickering to Grosmont (by agreement with British Rail and North York Moors Railway), got lost in dense forest plantations, scrambled in disused quarries and discovered hidden pockets of unimproved grassland. Proof-reading of the text has been undertaken by Liz Smith whose suggestions and corrections have been welcomed and incorporated.

Chris Wilson (manager of the Cornfield Flower Project at Ryedale Folk Museum, Hutton-le-Hole) has lived up to his reputation for finding and recording rarities and endangered species, often providing transport as well as guidance to difficult sites.

Mike Yates (Botanical Recorder for Whitby Naturalists' Club) and Cedric Gillings (Botanical Recorder for Scarborough Field Naturalists' Society) have drawn on detailed local plant knowledge and trawled historical records to produce status and site data. Alan Ritson scaled fragile coastal cliffs for rare plants. Vincent Jones (Botanical Recorder for VC62*) confiirmed the current status and whereabouts of uncommon species.

Further contributions in various ways have been made by Jenny Bartlett, Tom and Janet Denney, Bob and Jenny Dicker, Alan Dyson, Tamar Jones, Jill Magee, Pauline Popely, Ken Trewren and Brian Walker; also by ecologists at the North York Moors National Park Authority, Ryedale and Scarborough District Councils and the Howardian Hills AONB. Plant records have been obtained from the North & East York Ecological Data Centre, Sleights Botanical Group, the Yorkshire Naturalists' Union, the Botanical Society of the British Isles, the Forestry Commission and the Pannett Museum, Whitby.

My grateful thanks go to all who have helped to produce this book.

*VC62. For botanical recording, the British Isles is divided into areas known as vice counties; 62 extends across the area covered by this book.

Photos by Nan Sykes except where named.

HABITATS

While a small number of plants manage to grow almost anywhere, the vast majority are quite specific regarding the habitat in which they thrive, requiring particular soils, aspect, nutrients, temperature range and moisture. Summarised below are the major local habitats, but within each, wide variations produce many micro-habitats and scope for unexpected species to grow. Plant distribution and survival are never static, influenced both by changes of land use and natural forces – and changes will become increasingly noticeable as global warming increases.

FORESTS

When the Forestry Commission was established in 1919, its policy was to replace old deciduous species-rich woodland with fast-growing conifer plantations to provide a timber resource for the nation. In the late C20th this policy was replaced with deciduous woodland restoration to enhance wildlife and make forests more visually acceptable and accessible – a long-term plan which can be seen developing in the North Riding Forest Park centred at Dalby. Although wild flowers cannot survive inside a dense conifer plantation, the countless wood edges, access roads, tracks and streamsides provide habitats for a wide variety of species including uncommon *knotted pearlwort, hawkweeds, golden rod, slender St. John's-wort, fragrant agrimony* and *common centaury.* Disused quarries, subject to minimum disturbance, host *viper's-bugloss, autumn gentian, ploughman's-spikenard, fly, bee* and *common spotted orchids. Yellow bird's-nest,* a national rarity, has its only northern site in a Dalby Forest quarry; equally rare is *mountain everlasting* on a forest rock-outcrop. Wet areas remain undrained to the benefit of *narrow-leaved marsh orchid, marsh helleborine* and *meadow rue;* meadowland by Staindale water sustains *great burnet* amidst a colourful array of less common grassland species.

Over centuries, plant hunters sent home seeds of new species from around the world. Exotic conifers are maturing in some forest plantations, but the introduction of *Rhododendron ponticum* has created a major and expensive problem with its ability to spread rapidly and eliminate all other vegetation. It is being eradicated as resources allow.

BROAD-LEAVED WOODLAND

With endless variety of origin and historic management, no two woods are alike in their plant species. Richest are a few remnants of ancient woodland (areas believed to have had continuous tree cover of some sort since 1600 AD, and therefore likely to have been part of the original post-glacial wildwood) where the long-established ground flora may include *baneberry, herb paris, lily-of-the-valley, wintergreen* or *mountain currant*. By contrast, in woods used for pheasant-rearing scarcely any ground flora survives. Between these extremes, deciduous woodland is vibrant in the spring with early-flowering species, to be replaced by a variety of shade-tolerant plants as the leaf canopy unfolds.

Of particular note in this area are veteran trees; some oaks in *Duncombe Park* are thought to be nearly 1,000 years old.

On more calcareous soils on the Tabular Hills along the southern moorland edge and on the Howardian Hills, **ash and oak woods** support a mixture of *hazel, field maple, wych elm, wild privet, spindle, cherry* and *small-leaved lime*. Ground flora might include:
*aquilegia or columbine,
baneberry
bird's nest orchid
broad-leaved helleborine
common wintergreen
dog's mercury
early purple orchid
giant bellflower
golden saxifrages
goldilocks
greater butterfly orchid
herb-paris
lily-of-the-valley
moschatel
ramsons or wild garlic
sweet woodruff
sanicle
spurge laurel
tutsan
twayblade
violets
wood anemone
wood vetch
wood speedwell
wood sorrel
yellow archangel
yellow pimpernel
yellow-star-of-Bethlehem*

Wet woodland is a feature of the Howardian Hills. A mosaic of water, wet peat and drier hummocks provides habitat for *crack* and other *willows, alder, downy birch* and perhaps *aspen, hawthorn* and *guelder rose;* various marsh plants, including colonies of *marsh marigold* and impressive stands of tall sedges, often dominate the understorey.

In **dalehead woods**, mainly on acidic soils, *hybrid* and *sessile oaks, birch, rowan* and *holly* are likely, perhaps with:
*bilberry
bluebells
brambles
chickweed-wintergreen
climbing corydalis
cow-wheat
honeysuckle
wild daffodils
wood anemone
wood sage
wood sorrel*

MOORLAND

bell heather
bilberry
bog asphodel
bog pimpernel
butterwort
bog rosemary
bracken
chickweed-wintergreen
cottongrasses
cowberry
cranberry
cross-leaved heath
crowfoots
crowberry
creeping willow
dwarf cornel
heather or ling
marsh violet
milkwort
New Zealand willowherb
pale forget-me-not
petty whin
sundew
sweet gale
tormentil

The famous panorama of heather-clad moorland, stretching 33 miles(53km) from the coast to the western escarpment, and 13 miles(20km) north to south, is the largest continuous stretch of heather moorland in England and Wales, and was the main reason for designation in 1952 of the North York Moors National Park. For more than 5,000 years man increasingly removed woodland and scrub, leaving exposed soils to degrade under fire, cultivation and a harsh climate, and opening the way for acid-tolerant plants — mainly *common heather (ling)* which had been an undershrub in the original wildwood. Today, natural reversion to woodland is checked by sheep grazing and rotational heather burning or cutting to support red grouse populations. Despite a plateau vista, walkers soon realise that the moorland is no uniform landscape, but is criss-crossed by rivulets, streams, bogs, charred remains of recent fires and steep-sided dales. Where springs emerge on the moors or rivulets meander, fan-shaped flushes of slow-moving water provide habitat for specialised species such as *round-leaved sundew* and *butterwort* which supplement their nutrient-poor habitat by trapping insects. In more permanent water, bright yellow-flowering patches of *bog asphodel* are less frequent than aromatic colonies of *sweet gale. Dwarf cornel,* an arctic plant, clings to north-facing slopes at the *Hole of Horcum.* Other glacial relics — *bog rosemary* and *cloudberry* — survive in small numbers at *May Moss,* north of *Saltergate.* Remnants of once widespread heathland in the Howardian Hills occur in a few conifer plantations near *Yearsley* and *Grimston.*

WETLAND

As the last ice age, with its massive glaciers gripping North East Yorkshire, receded approximately 12,000 years ago, open water and marshland spread across the Vale of Pickering, Eskdale and associated valleys. Much of this land has since been drained to form productive farmland, crossed by rivers Esk, Rye and Derwent with their network of feeder streams and ditches. Despite two centuries of drainage schemes, including re-alignment of river channels on the Hertford and Derwent, the building of dams, mill leats and flood prevention schemes, marsh plants are plentiful along stream sides, in lakes, ponds and waterlogged pastures. Man-made lakes such as Newburgh Priory, Castle Howard, Scaling Dam, Oulston, Throxenby Mere and Burton Riggs, along with worked out gravel pits and reservoirs provide more wetland habitats; on a smaller scale are numerous ponds created for wildfowl or visual amenity.

Although most wetland species have stable populations, a few such as *water violet, pink water speedwell, flowering rush* and *lesser water plantain* struggle against the demands of drainage schemes. A rare colony of *tufted loosestrife* fringes Lake Gormire, a natural ice-age legacy at the foot of Sutton Bank escarpment; *bladderwort* grows in Gilling Lakes, *meadow rue* on Flixton Carr, *marsh St.John's-wort* at Sheepwash and on Spaunton moor; *bird's-eye primrose* around Arden and Rievaulx; *marsh helleborine* near Dalby and *globe flower* in Newton*dale. Marsh gentian,* last seen near Cropton in the 1980's, is believed to be locally extinct after land drainage. Ironically the watery landscape contains three alien introductions for which extinction would be welcome; *Himalayan balsam* is steadily swamping riversides; *New Zealand pigmyweed* and *floating pennywort* are aggressive pond invaders.

angelica
arrowgrasses
bedstraws
bird's-eye primrose
bogbean
bur-reed
butterbur
celery-lvd buttercup
common fleabane
cuckoo flower
figworts
fool's watercress
globe flower
golden saxifrages
grass-of-Parnassus
gypsywort
large bittercress
lesser water-parsnip
mare's-tail
marsh cinquefoil
marsh hawk's-beard
marsh helleborine
marsh lousewort
marsh marigold
marsh orchids
marsh pennywort
marsh ragwort
marsh St John's-wort
meadow rue
meadowsweet
monkeyflower
pondweeds
ragged robin
reedmace
skullcap
sneezewort
stitchworts
tufted loosestrife
valerians
watercress
water crowfoots
water forget-me-nots
water lilies
water milfoil
water mint
water plantain
water speedwells
water violet
willowherbs
yellow flag

GRASSLAND

Soil type and management systems determine grassland species. On highly productive farmland, where maximum herbage is needed for grazing or silage making, grassland is likely to be heavily fertilised and re-seeded at intervals. *Ryegrass* and *white clover* may dominate the sward. Infrequently on farmland, verges, wasteland, light scrub, awkward field corners or churchyards are small herb-rich remnants of limestone grassland. Ellerburn Bank, a Yorkshire Wildlife Trust reserve north of Thornton-le-Dale, is managed to maintain this type of pasture. But between these extremes, grassy places are infinitely variable with ever-changing plant communities. The lists indicate species preferences.

On **coastal grassy cliffs** *yellow-wort, restharrow, wild carrot* and *kidney vetch* are frequent. Wet grassy slopes, with perhaps *common fleabane, meadow saxifrage, grass-of-Parnassus* and *hemp agrimony,* may merge into marsh with *bulrush, ragged robin* and *hemlock water-dropwort.*

Sandy grassland along the southern edge of the Vale of Pickering has:
bird's-foot	prickly poppy
common cudweed	hare's-foot clover
forget-me-nots	smooth cat's-ear
changing	spring vetch
early	knotted clover

On acidic or neutral soils:
betony
bird's-foot trefoil
bitter vetchling
bugle
buttercups
cat's-ear
clovers
crosswort
docks
eyebright
harebell
hawkbits
knapweed
meadow vetchling
mouse-ear
orchids
ox-eye daisy
pignut
plantains
St.John's-worts
scabious
sorrels
stitchworts
thistles
tormentil
yellow rattle

On calcareous soils:
burnet-saxifrage
cowslip
greater knapweed
dropwort
field mouse-ear
hairy violet
hoary plantain
lady's bedstraw
marjoram
orchids, burnt
fragrant
pyramidal
fly
bee
butterfly
pepper-saxifrage
rockrose
St.John's-wort
salad-burnet
saw-wort
scabious
thistles, carline
musk
woolly
wild basil
wild carrot
wild thyme

VERGES

An extensive network of roads, tracks and lanes, usually with verges on both sides, spreads across grassland, woodland, wetland, farmland and moor, providing infinite variety of habitat for common species, and importantly, for survival of plants which have become rare elsewhere in today's managed countryside. Continuity of verges and their edgings of ditch, hedge or wall create essential corridors along which wildlife can spread to maintain viable populations.

Traditionally road verges were lightly-grazed by village livestock or cut for hay, but modern mechanised management, prompted by the need for minimum maintenance and a 'tidy at any price' outlook, tends to destroy this important resource together with dependent insects, butterflies and bees. Increasingly a compromise is practised, whereby a road edge swathe is cut regularly to ensure road safety, and further back from the road is cut less frequently, allowing plants to flower and seed while controlling robust perennials and woody species.

Verges are a refuge for once abundant wild flowers such as *cowslip, primrose, giant bellflower* and *meadow crane's-bill,* while rarities such as *stone bramble, common wintergreen* and *broad-leaved helleborine,* are almost totally reliant on verges for their survival.

On roads subject to winter salt-spraying, saltmarsh plants such as *sea spurreys, danish scurvygrass* and *oraches* fringe the roadside splash zone. Moorland verges are often tightly sheep-grazed, but with more robust species constantly nibbled, numerous smaller plants including *eyebright, dog violets, medicks, milkwort, crane's-bills, plantains, clovers* and *knotted-pearlwort* create a dense mat of miniature plants.

Species more frequent on verges than elsewhere:
agrimony
butterburs
coltsfoot
comfrey
common spotted
  orchid
cow parsley
cowslip
dandelions
field scabious
goat's-beard
greater
  burnet-saxifrage
hedge parsley
hedge woundwort
hogweed
meadow crane's-bill
meadow vetchling
moschatel
primrose
red bartsia
rough chervil
rough hawk's-beard
sweet cicely
sowthistles
tansy
vetches
violets
wild arum
wild basil
yarrow

Tiered cutting retains native wildflowers

Wildlife not welcome

HEDGEROWS

Hedgerows may originate from remnant ancient wildwood or from field boundaries planted during the enclosure era of c.1750-1850, or from recent plantings under conservation schemes to redress widespread hedgerow removal during the C20th. Alongside fields and roads, hedges are normally maintained by mechanical cutting at a height of approximately 4ft (1.25m) with occasional marked tree saplings left to grow to maturity. Older hedges are likely to be sinuous, with greater species variety, and less common shrubs like *dogwood, purging buckthorn* or *sweet briar*. When the centuries-old communal open field system gave way to land enclosure for individual ownership, straight hedgerows were laid out in a grid pattern.

These were usually planted with *hawthorn,* occasionally *blackthorn, elm, holly* or *hazel,* and have been augmented since by *gooseberry, roses, teaplant, snowberry* and other bird-sown shrubs. Some species such as *toothwort,* parasitic on hazel or elm, are more frequent at the base of hedgerows than elsewhere; hedgerows are used by climbers such as *black bryony, bindweeds, honeysuckle* and *ivy* with *wood vetch* near the coast.

ash
elm
black bryony
blackthorn
dogwood
elder
field maple
gooseberry
guelder rose
hawthorn
hazel
holly
ivy
roses
snowberry
teaplant
wild privet
white bryony
wood vetch

WALLS & QUARRIES & ROCKS

Stony outcrops, disused quarries and walls attract plants able to cope with dehydration. *Wallflower* adorns several abbey and castle ruins but the dainty *fairy foxglove* seems limited to *Helmsley Castle* and *Mount Grace Priory*. Despite occasional stone cleaning, small plants of *eastern rocket* survive on *Byland Abbey; pellitory-of-the-wall* is plentiful near *Whitby Abbey,* also at *Scarborough Castle* where *common calamint* and *spotted medick* flourish but *wild clary,* at its only known local site, struggles to survive. Where limestone quarries have long been abandoned and not used for rubbish tipping, the flora reflects local seed availability and may include rarities such as *pale St John's-wort,* Bithynian vetch, ploughman's-spikenard, hairy rockcress* and *bloody cranesbill*.

Bithynian vetch
bloody cranesbill
fairy foxglove
hairy rockcress
ivy-leaved toadflax
mouse-ear hawkweed
pale St.John's wort
pellitory-of-the-wall
red valerian
rue-leaved saxifrage
spring whitlowgrass
thale-cress
thyme
wall lettuce
wallflower
stonecrops

ARABLE LAND

The opportunist, mainly annual, wild flowers which for centuries were a colourful yet troublesome part of cultivated farmland, have diminished dramatically in recent decades, due to modern farming practices. Several are listed as critically on the edge of extinction. Locally these include *cornflower, red hemp-nettle, corn buttercup, treacle mustard, Venus's looking-glass* and *corn gromwell. Corncockle* is locally extinct in the wild. At Ryedale Folk Museum, Hutton-le-Hole, a nursery and cornfield have been established to sustain endangered species while encouraging farmers to establish conservation flower-rich headlands.

black bindweed	mayweeds
bugloss	night-flowering
charlock	catchfly
corn buttercup	pale persicaria
cornfield knotgrass	pennycress
cornflower	pansies
corn mint	poppies
cornsalads	red hempnettle
corn spurrey	redshank
deadnettles	scarlet pimpernel
dwarf spurge	sharp-leaved fluellen
field madder	shepherd's needle
field woundwort	speedwells
flixweed	treacle mustard
fumitories	venus's looking-glass
fool's parsley	wild radish

SEASHORE AND CLIFFS

Seaweed-clad boulders and wave-scoured rocks occupy much of the coastal tidal zone. Intervening sandy shores have opportunist plants of *sea milkwort, sea sandwort, sea rocket, saltwort* and *oraches*. Saltmarshes on the coast are limited to ever-reducing areas of the Esk estuary between Ruswarp and Whitby, where *sea aster, sea spurreys, sea arrowgrass* and *hemlock water-dropwort* struggle to survive against building development. By contrast coastal cliffs, largely formed from eroding boulder clay, and ever at risk from cliff erosion, offer a variety of locations readily colonised by diverse species, especially *grass-of-Parnassus and kidney vetch*. Water seepage and saline pools attract distinctive plant communities; wind-tolerant shrubs establish on drier, more stable cliffs.

alexanders	plantains
gum plant	primrose
coltsfoot	restharrow
grass-of-	scurvygrass
Parnassus	slender thistle
hoary ragwort	wild cabbage
kidney vetch	wild carrot
arrowgrass	wild celery
orchids	yellow-wort

TREES

SCOTS PINE *Pinus sylvestris*

Widespread in small groups or solitary on moorland fringe and in plantations. Can reach 50m tall; bark orange/brown, scaly; leaves narrow, 5-7cm long, in pairs, greyish and slightly twisted.

mature cones   young cones

YEW *Taxus baccata*

Long-lived native and poisonous evergreen; seedlings naturalise easily from traditional plantings in churchyards and parks.
Up to 25m tall with dark green, shiny, linear foliage. Male flowers shed pollen Feb-Apr; female flowers tiny, mature into red fruits Sep-Oct.

fruit   male flowers

JUNIPER *Juniperus communis*

Rare moorland shrub or small tree up to 15m high, formerly more widespread. Its current reluctance to regenerate naturally has prompted a programme to propagate from local cuttings and plant seedlings. Male cones shed pollen in March; female cones ripen in the 2nd or 3rd year and mature from green to black; m and f cones usually on separate bushes.

♀
♂

HOLLY *Ilex aquifolium*

Small evergreen tree common in woods, scrub and often a hedgerow shrub. **Leaves** dark glossy green, leathery, wavy-edged, most with sharp spines; **flowers** May-Aug, 4-6mm across, 4 white petals, male and female on separate trees; familiar red berries develop late in the year.

LARCH *Larix sp*

Deciduous conifer common in plantations, frequently self-sown. About 40m tall with greyish fissured bark; **leaves** light green, soft and short, in clusters, turn golden in autumn before leaf-fall. Stubby male cones shed pollen in April as female cones enlarge. Both Common and Japanese larch have been planted; the hybrid is most frequent.

WYCH ELM *Ulmus glabra*

A broad tree up to 40m tall frequent in hedgerows, open woods and copses. Rarely produces suckers. **Leaf** hairy, has unequal base almost overlapping the hairy stalk. Dense purplish flower clusters Feb-Mar; oval winged fruits.

ENGLISH ELM *Ulmus procera* is rarely seen as a mature tree following Dutch elm disease. It survives mainly as hedgerow regrowth. Unlike wych elm it produces numerous suckers.

ASH *Fraxinus excelsior*

Abundant in hedgerows, woods, cliffs and scree, especially on base-rich soils; native deciduous tree to 40m tall; angular branching, usually up-turned ends; sooty black buds. **Flowers** Mar-May, tufts of purple stamens, no petals; pinnate **leaves** unfold after flowers; long-winged fruits hang in bunches.

ASPEN *Populus tremula*

Occasional short-lived tree up to 20m tall in copses and road-sides, suckers create small colonies. **Leaves** wavy-edged, greyish above, pale below, have flattened stalk which causes the blade to flutter continuously. Thick male catkins and long female catkins on same tree in March.

PURGING BUCKTHORN *Rhamnus cathartica*

Deciduous shrub or small tree to 10m tall; locally scarce, grows in scrub woodland or hedgerow on limestone. **Leaves** show parallel veins converging at the tip and neatly serrated edge. **Flowers** May-Jun, fragrant, tiny, greenish, male and female on separate bushes; fruit black, rapidly purging if eaten.

OAKS *Quercus spp*

Long-lived rugged trees up to 40m tall, common in wood and hedgerow. Hanging catkins emerge with leaves May-Jun; female and long male separate on same tree; acorns ripen in October. Veteran oaks up to 1,000 years old survive near *Helmsley*.

Pedunculate oak (*Quercus robur*) has stalked acorns; leaves ± stalkless and lobed at base.

Sessile oak (*Quercus petraea*) has stalkless acorns; leaves hairy, stalked, tapering at base.

Hybrids are widespread.

LIME *Tilia spp* Large deciduous trees; small off-white, slightly scented, 5-petalled flowers Jun-Jul, in bunches, stalked from pale papery bract; **leaves** coloured a distinctive 'lime-green', very obvious in the spring; fruit is a small hard, oval nut.

Small-leaved Lime *Tilia cordata*
Native tree, infrequent in old deciduous woodland. Under-leaf hair tufts brown; flower sprays held <u>horizontally or upright.</u>
Large-leaved Lime *Tilia platyphyllos*
Rare native tree, occasionally planted; fruits downy.
Common Lime *Tilia x europaea*
A widely planted hybrid between small and large leaved limes; white under-leaf hair tufts; flower sprays <u>hang down.</u>

BEECH *Fagus sylvatica*
Deciduous spreading tree up to 45m tall. Doubtfully native in this area but often planted. Slender pointed buds; **leaves** open pale green, turn golden brown, softly hairy when young; fringed catkins, separate male and female on same tree; 1 or 2 shiny brown nuts in woody case.

BIRCH *Betula sp*

♂

♀

Common pioneer, short-lived trees up to 30m tall on light or poor soils, avoiding deep shade; m and f catkins on the same tree Apr-May. The two local species frequently hybridise.

Silver birch
(*B.pendula*)
White papery
bark, drooping
branches.

Downy birch
(*B.pubescens*)
Grey/brown
bark, branches
spreading.

ALDER *Alnus glutinosa*

Common wetland tree grows to 20m tall. Abundant alongside rivers and streams. Catkins - male hanging and female stubby, Feb-Mar, before the leaves; buds purple; green f. cones dry brown, woody, and persist on the tree throughout the winter.

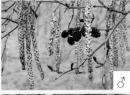
♂

♀

HAZEL *Corylus avellana*

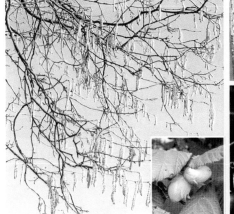

♀

♂

Common hedgerow shrub or small tree to 6m. Hanging m. catkins and tiny red tufted f. catkins appear early spring before the leaves. Edible hazelnuts ripen through the autumn.

SYCAMORE *Acer pseudoplatanus*

Deciduous spreading tree to 30m; common in woodland, hedges, fields; hanging flower clusters May-Jun.

NORWAY MAPLE *Acer platanoides* is a deciduous introduction, frequently planted and self-sown in hedgerow and amenity areas; differs from sycamore by its thinner leaves, more pointed leaf lobes and ± erect flower spray.

FIELD MAPLE *Acer campestre*

Small deciduous tree to 20m; frequent in open woodland and as a hedgerow shrub on basic soils; erect flower sprays May-Jun; leaves bright yellow in spring, turn gold or red in autumn.

HORSE CHESTNUT *Aesculus hippocastanum*

Deciduous introduction planted in parks, streets and village greens, occasionally self-sown. Buds brown, sticky; flowers white/pink May-Jun; a spiny shell encloses a nut or 'conquer'.

Willows are deciduous trees or shrubs, usually growing on moist ground. Flowers appear from March (goat willow) to June (bay willow); they are small, usually with 2 stamens, held in catkins, male and female on separate trees; white shiny male catkins with bright yellow stamens often known as 'pussy willow'; less prominent female catkins are grey/green; frequent hybridisation between species. Leaves are a better identification feature than catkins.

WHITE WILLOW
Salix alba
A waterside tree with slender, pointed, leaves, finely tooth-edged and covered with silvery white hairs, especially beneath. Catkins in May.

OSIER *Salix viminalis*
Med-tall non-native shrub with long flexible ginger twigs once used for basket weaving; very long narrow leaves, green above, white hairy beneath.

BAY WILLOW
Salix pentandra
Large shrub with dark green leaves, shiny, sticky and fragrant; long, slender male catkins flowers have 5 bright yellow stamens, May-Jun.

CRACK WILLOW *Salix fragilis agg*
On wet ground or by riverside, a spreading, rather untidy tree with branches which easily snap off. Leaves bright green above, pale beneath, asymmetrical at the tip. Catkins Apr-May, with the leaves.

GOAT WILLOW
Salix caprea
Common shrub to 10m, on wet and dry ground; leaves broad oval, paler beneath, feel soft; hairless when mature. 'Pussy willow' catkins before leaves.

GREY WILLOW
Salix cinerea
Frequent shrub on damp ground; leaves oval, pointed, inrolled edges, brown and white hairs beneath. Catkins Mar-Apr, usually before leaves.

EARED WILLOW
Salix aurita
Small shrub, common on moorland and acid wet ground; leaves wrinkled with wavy, inrolled edges; large 'ear-like' stipules on stem. Catkins slender, Apr-May, before the leaves.

CREEPING WILLOW
Salix repens agg
Variable, low sprawling or prostrate moorland shrublet; leaves small, rounded or pointed, with fine, silvery hairs beneath. Catkins short, Apr-May, before leaves.

BUTTERCUP FAMILY   RANUNCULACEAE

A variable group of plants, primitive in evolutionary term   s; most have flowers with num   erous stamens and 5 petals or petaloid sepals, often with nectar-secreting organs at the base.

CREEPING BUTTERCUP
Ranunculus repens
Common in grassy places, pathsides, verges and waste ground, avoiding only very acidic soils. Flowers   May-Oct, shiny 10-15mm diam;stems furrowed, erect 20-60cm;   leaves hairy 3-lobed, the centre lobe stalked; extensive rooting runners.

MEADOW BUTTERCUP
Ranunculus acris
Common in old grassland except on very acidic or dry soils. Flowers   Apr-Oct, shiny 15-25mm diam on round stems 30-100cm tall, branched and hairy but not ridged; leaves palmate, toothed and hairy; no underground runners.

BULBOUS BUTTERCUP
Ranunculus bulbosus
A frequent early-flowering buttercup on drier grassy areas; prefers a lime-rich soil. Flowers   Apr-Jun, 20-30mm, on hairy furrowed stalks; sepals reflexed; leaves   hairy, toothed with stalked middle lobe; upper leaves more linear; stem 5-40 cm has bulbous base; no runners.

CORN or PERENNIAL BUTTERCUP
Ranunculus arvensis
A sprawling, hairy annual, with stems up to 60cm. Rare on arable land. **Flowers** Jun-Jul, 4-12mm, petals bright yellow, sepals erect, slender; **leaves** have narrow linear segments, some forked; large **fruits** have clusters of achenes with prominent straight spines.

HAIRY BUTTERCUP
Ranunculus sardous
A sprawling, late-flowering annual, rare in this area where it reaches its northern UK limit; prefers damp soils. **Flowers** Jun-Oct, 12-25mm, 5 or more pale yellow petals; sepals reflexed; stems hairy 10-45cm; **leaves** hairy, shiny, 3-lobed, toothed, centre lobe stalked; linear upper stem leaves.

GOLDILOCKS *Ranunculus auricomus*
A patch-forming perennial, occasional in light woodland, scrub and grassy road verges. **Flowers** Apr-May, likely to have mis-shapen or no petals; sepals hairy, dark-tipped; **leaves** from the base long-stalked roundish, lobed, crenate edged; upper leaves ± sessile, linear; stems erect 10-40 cm, branched, downy.

SMALL-FLOWERED BUTTERCUP
Ranunculus parviflorus
At its northern limit, rare sprawling short annual on lime-rich bare or grassy ground. **Flowers** Jun-Aug, pale yellow, only 3-5mm, often with missing petals; small down-turned sepals; **leaves** lobed near the base, ovate up the stem, all hairy.

MARSH MARIGOLD *Caltha palustris*

Also known as kingcup or water blob, this common wetland perennial grows in large colonies in a variety of habitats - streams, ponds, wet meadows, alder carr. Stout fleshy stems up to 60cm produce large leafy clumps. **Flowers** Apr-Jul, golden yellow 15-50mm; **leaves** large shiny, kidney-shaped with serrated edges.

CELERY-LEAVED BUTTERCUP
Ranunculus sceleratus
Unusual annual in shallow, still or slow-moving water or muddy ground enriched by standing cattle. Salt-tolerant, it also occurs in stagnant tidal pools. **Flowers** May-Sep, pale yellow, only 5-10mm; **leaves** shiny with narrow pointed lobes like celery; stems ridged, hollow, much branched; **fruit** an elongated head of achenes.

GLOBE FLOWER
Trollius europaeus
An upland species, its population has diminished with increasing land drainage. Survives infrequently in waterlogged land, also in non-grazed disused limestone quarries. **Flowers** Jun-Aug, usually solitary on erect leafy stems to 60cm; up to 10 yellow sepals curve inward forming a 2-3cm globe and enclosing nectar-secreting petals and many stamens; **leaves**

Spearworts are hairless perennials in wetland, patch-forming with creeping stems and spear-shaped leaves.

LESSER SPEARWORT
Ranunculus flammula

Widespread in marshy meadows, shallow streams, bogs and pools, often amongst other vegetation. Extensive rooting runners give rise to hollow, furrowed stems up to 50cm, upright or trailing. **Flowers** Jun-Oct, pale yellow, 7-18mm; **leaves** grass-like, slightly toothed.

GREATER SPEARWORT
Ranunculus lingua

Rare, mainly planted in ornamental lakes and ponds; can form large showy colonies with flowering stems a metre or more tall. **Flowers** Jun-Aug, bright yellow, 20-50mm; long spear-shaped stem **leaves**; submerged leaves oval, disappear before flowering.

LESSER CELANDINE   *Ranunculus ficaria*

Common low-growing and abundant perennial found in a wide range of habitats - fields, woods, hedgebanks, streamsides, gardens - usually on damp, disturbed or grassy ground.

Extensive spreads result from plants with rooting stems or basal bulbils *(ssp bulbifera)*. **Flowers** Mar-May, 20-30mm, single on stems to 20cm; 6-12 bright yellow, shiny petals (soon fade white), 3 sepals; **leaves** cordate, often mottled, on long stalks.

WINTER ACONITE   *Eranthis hyemalis*

An east European plant introduced in the C16th, has naturalised in gardens, light woodland and on village greens.

Low-growing from underground tubers, it creates extensive carpets in early spring. **Flowers** Jan-Mar, cup-shaped c.25mm, solitary on short, hollow, hairless stems; 6 large yellow sepals surround 6 tiny petals and clusters of yellow stamens; **leafy bracts** form a green ruff beneath the flower; glossy divided root leaves appear after flowering.

Water Crowfoots are white-flowered buttercups growing in water or damp ground. Size of flower, leaf shape and nectaries at base of petals are guides to species identification, made difficult by hybridisation.

IVY-LEAVED CROWFOOT *R.hederaceus*
Almost prostrate on mud, our smallest crowfoot

with **flowers** Jun-Sep, 4-8mm across; sepals show between spaced petals; **leaves** 3 or 5 lobed, widest near leaf stalk. Occasional in shallow water or mud, especially where cattle stand.

ROUND-LEAVED CROWFOOT *R.omiophyllus*
Low-growing short-lived plant of acidic pools,

shallow ditches, gate- ways and moorland flushes avoiding lime-rich water. **Leaves** round scallop-edged, narrowed near the stalk; **flowers** Jun-Aug, 10-12mm, petals cover the sepals.

SHORT-LEAVED WATER-CROWFOOT *R.trichophyllus*
Early-flowering small crowfoot occasional in shallow still or sluggish ditches and ponds, usually away from the hills. It has no floating leaves; submerged leaves finely divided into short, hair-like strands; **flowers** May-Jun, about 10mm, floating or just above the water surface, on curved stalks ± equal length to the leaves.

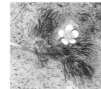

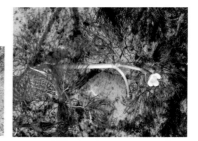

COMMON WATER-CROWFOOT *R.aquatilis*
POND WATER-CROWFOOT *R. peltatus*
Two similar annuals or perennials growing in ponds, ditches and streamsides. Submerged leaves finely divided into linear segments; floating leaves cut into lobes, toothed at the end, but not always present; **flowers** May-Aug, usually less than 10mm in *R.aquatilis* which has circular nectaries, and 10-30mm in *R.peltatus* which has pear-shaped nectaries.

LONG-LEAVED WATER-CROWFOOT
R.penicillatus subsp.pseudofluitans
RIVER WATER-CROWFOOT *R.fluitans*
Two much confused robust crowfoots quite frequent in fast-flowing streams and rivers. Stems have divided linear leaves up to 2m long which flow with the current. Floating leaves rarely present. **Flowers** May-Aug, variable, 20-30mm often held well above the water surface.

BANEBERRY *Actaea spicata*
Also known as Herb Christopher, a low bushy perennial with a strange UK distribution, growing only in parts of Yorkshire, Lancashire and Cumbria. Small but stable populations in shady scrubland or ashwoods on limestone rock south of the moors. Stems to 45cm. **Flowers** May-Jul, in loose clusters, small creamy white with many projecting stamens; **leaves** segmented, unevenly toothed; **fruits** green then shiny black berries, poisonous.

COLUMBINE *Aquilegia vulgaris*
Infrequent hairless perennial in shady scrub and woodland glades on lime-rich soils. Slender stems to 1m tall. **Flowers** Jun-Jul, have 5 spurred sepals and 5 petals, all dark purple; **leaves** thin, greyish in 3 lobed segments. (Garden varieties have large pale blue, white or pink flowers with long spurs).

GREEN HELLEBORE *Helleborus viridis*
Once used as a cottage vermifuge, this plant has small native populations where it prefers light shade on limestone; frequently planted in gardens. **Flowers** Feb-Apr, 3-5cm, 5 green petal-like sepals; several flowers on thick-stemmed leafy clumps to 40cm tall; **leaves** tough, dark green in large lobed segments, long-stalked basal. Dies back in winter.

STINKING HELLEBORE *Helleborus foetidus*
A foetid perennial of calcareous rocky outcrops and woodland glades; often planted in gardens and churchyards. **Flowers** Mar-Apr, cup-shaped 1-3cm across; petal-like sepals yellow/green bordered purple; robust stems up to 80cm have **leaves** ± evergreen, with long narrow segments, tooth-edged; no stalked basal leaves.

WOOD ANEMONE
Anemone nemorosa
Early and abundant
springtime perennial,
covers the ground in old
woodland; more sparse on
meadows and hedgebanks.
Flowers Mar-May, 20-
40mm, solitary on slender
stems 10 to 30cm tall;
petals white often suffused
pink; **leaves** both halfway
up the stem and long-
stalked from the ground, all
lobed.

MONK'S-HOOD
Aconitum napellus
A showy poisonous
perennial, infrequent on
shady streamsides and
wood edge. Origin obscure,
local plants likely to be
garden escapes. Stems to
1.5m tall. **Flowers** May-
Sep, helmet-shaped with 2
nectar-secreting spurs,
blue/purple; **leaves** short-
stalked up the stem,
divided into narrow
segments.

TRAVELLER'S JOY
Clematis vitalba
Infrequent at its northern
limit, scrambles on walls,
fences, mainly by the
coast. **Flowers** Jul-Aug,
10-20mm,fragrant, on
woody stems up to 30m
long; **leaves** have 3-5
broad, pointed leaflets;
fruits with pale whitish
hairy plumes give rise to its
other name of 'old man's
beard'.

COMMON MEADOW RUE
Thalictrum flavum
Rare in fens, wet woodland
and riverside with base-rich
water. An elegant perennial
with furrowed stems to 1m
tall, often amidst other
robust wetland vegetation.
Flowers Jul-Aug, small
creamy white with many
yellow stamens in stalked
terminal clusters; **leaves**
cut into several narrow
wedge-shaped segments.

BOG MYRTLE FAMILY   *MYRICACEAE*

BOG MYRTLE or SWEET GALE   *Myrica gale*
An aromatic deciduous moorland shrub from which leaves are gathered to flavour home-brewed gale beer. Covers large boggy upland areas with 2m tall bushes. **Flowers** Apr-May, stubby male catkins, yellow turning to copper with red stamens; round female catkins with red styles, usually on separate plants; **leaves** greyish green, downy beneath, pitted with resinous aromatic glands.

♂

♀

fruit

FUMITORY FAMILY   *FUMARIACEAE*

Scrambling, rather fragile plants with waxy deeply-divided hairless leaves; small tubular flowers comprise 2 tiny sepals, 2 outer petals, 2 inner petals and 2 stamens.

CLIMBING CORYDALIS   *Ceratocapnos claviculata*
Sprawling low slender annual on free-draining acidic

or peaty soils; frequent on felled plantations, in light woodland and amongst bracken; clambers widely with tendrils. **Flowers** May-Sep, creamy white 5-6mm long, few in short open spikes; **leaves** have small greyish leaflets and thin coiling tendrils.

YELLOW CORYDALIS   *Pseudofumaria lutea*
An alpine perennial grown in UK gardens and widely

naturalised in old mortared walls and stony crevices; forms dense clumps up to 30cm high; has no tendrils. **Flowers** May-Sep, deep yellow 12-10mm long on terminal spikes; **leaves** have thin, short-stalked lobed leaflets.

COMMON FUMITORY *Fumaria officinalis*

Common on arable land. A weak sprawling annual to 20cm tall and often much wider. **Flowers** Apr-Oct, 6-8mm long, pink, darker at the tip, on terminal spikes; **leaves** have greyish leaflets cleft into flat lobes.

FINE-LEAVED FUMITORY *Fumaria parviflora*

A rare scrambling annual amongst spring-sown crops on calcareous arable fields and bare ground. **Flowers** Jun-Sep, less than 6mm long, white slightly pink-tinged; **leaves** cut into narrow short leaflets.

COMMON RAMPING FUMITORY *Fumaria muralis*

Despite its name, locally uncommon, mostly confined to a few coastal sites. Scrambles on hedge banks and arable land with acidic free-draining soils. **Flowers** May-Oct, 9-11mm, up to 15 flowers per spike, pink with darker tip; <u>**fruit** stalk straight ± erect</u>.

WHITE RAMPING FUMITORY *Fumaria capreolata*

Plentiful on hedgerows and field edge near the coast, a vigorous scrambler over 2m high. **Flowers** May-Sep, 10-12mm long, up to 20 flowers per spike; creamy white with dark red tip; lowest petal narrow; <u>**fruit** stalk recurved</u>.

NETTLE FAMILY *URTICACEAE*

Small flowers with four-lobed green calyx, no petals; separate male and female flowers.

STINGING NETTLE *Urtica dioica*

Common perennial in damp, nutrient-rich ground, verges, gardens, and scrub. Stems square, erect to 1.5m, stinging hairs; spreads by yellow underground stems to create large 'nettle patches' attractive to butterflies. **Flowers** May-Sep, tiny 4-lobed, greenish; male and female in dangling catkins usually on separate plants; **leaves** toothed, pointed with stinging hairs.

SMALL NETTLE *Urtica urens*

Occasional annual on light disturbed fertile soils away from the hills. Stems 10-50cm tall have few hairs. Separate male and female **flowers** Jun-Sep, grow in short sprigs on the same plant; **leaves** oval shaped, deeply toothed and dark green, usually with few or no stinging hairs.

PELLITORY-OF-THE-WALL
Parietaria judaica
A softly hairy perennial, plentiful on old walls, buildings and exposed rocks, mainly along the coast, infrequent inland; abundant around *Whitby Abbey*. Stems branched, red, rooting at the nodes; **flowers** Jun-Oct, tiny, reddish, in clusters, female at stem tops, male lower down. **leaves** oval 7cm.

HOP FAMILY *CANNABACEAE*

HOP *Humulus lupulus*
Hairy square-stemmed perennial, climbs clockwise around poles, on hedges; formerly cultivated for brewing, naturalised in a few places. **Flowers** Jul-Sep, male in clusters, female like small pine cones enlarge in **fruit** to c.2cm.

♂   ♀

POPPY FAMILY *PAPAVERACEAE*

Herbs with solitary flowers; numerous stamens, 4 petals and 2 sepals which soon fall; stems contain latex - a milky or yellow juice; poppy seeds are dispersed through holes in a pepperpot type capsule.

FIELD POPPY
Papaver rhoeas

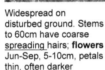

LONG-HEADED POPPY
Papaver dubium ssp.dubium

Widespread on disturbed ground. Stems to 60cm have coarse spreading hairs; **flowers** Jun-Sep, 5-10cm, petals thin, often darker towards the centre; **leaves** roughly hairy, long, pointed toothed leaflets; short smooth seed capsule.

Occasional on light land. Stems to 60cm with mainly appressed hairs, contain white latex; **flowers** Jun-Aug, 3-6cm, pale red, thin petals; **leaves** hairy, toothed; long narrow smooth capsule.

PRICKLY POPPY
P.argemone
A southern plant locally rare on sandy fields; long narrow bristly seed capsule and small, spaced petals.

P. dubium ssp.*lecoqii* differs from ssp.*dubium* by more spaced petals and latex which is yellow when exposed to air; also less hairy; sparse on lime-rich arable land.

WELSH POPPY *Meconopsis cambrica*

GREATER CELANDINE *Chelidonium majus*

Garden plant naturalised in small groups on verges and scrub, especially near villages. **Flowers** May-Aug, 5-7cm across, single on unbranched stems 30-60cm; thin yellow (or orange) petals; **leaves** scented, pale green, lobed and toothed; elongated capsule with domed lid.

Former medicinal plant, occasionally naturalised in large patches on scrub and verges near habitation. **Flowers** May-Sep, c.2.5cm across on branched stems to 1m; long thin many-seeded capsule; **leaves** thin, bluntly lobed, pale green.

GOOSEFOOT FAMILY *CHENOPODIACEAE*

A family of robust upright and sprawling plants with rather mealy, fleshy leaves and ridged, often red-striped stems; tiny obscure flowers with 5 sepals and no petals are clustered on spikes; fruits and leaf shape are the best means of identification. Frequent on wasteland or disturbed ground, many are salt-tolerant and thrive near the sea.

Goosefoots
(Chenopodium spp) have stamens and styles in the same flower; fruits are round, part enclosed by sepals.
(See oraches overleaf)

FAT-HEN
C.album
Common on roadside salt heaps and arable fields; branched annual 30-100cm tall. **Flowers** Jul-Oct, obscure in short greenish spikes; **leaves** pale with white mealy coating; pointed oval on upper stem, diamond shaped below.

RED GOOSEFOOT
C.rubrum
A large leafy annual, grows in quantity on manure heaps and nutrient-rich mud; ridged red-striped stems up to 1m tall. **Flowers** Jul-Oct, tiny, red-tinted in tight clusters on short spikes; **leaves** glossy dark green, irregularly-toothed, reddish beneath.

SEA BEET
Beta vulgaris
Occasional on nutrient-rich sea cliffs. **Flowers** Jun-Sep, tiny green/red, in clusters on long leafy spikes, **leaves** large, shiny, smaller near the tops of branched ridged stems up to 1m tall.

GOOD KING HENRY
C.bonus-henricus
Roman introduction, infrequent on grassy waste and near habitation; leafy perennial erect to 50cm. **Flowers** May-Jul, in dense clusters on leafless upper stem; **leaves** large triangular, wavy-edged; mealy when young, smooth green later.

PRICKLY SALTWORT
Salsola kali

Low sprawling annual grows infrequently on the tide-line of sandy shores. **Flowers** Jul-Oct, small 5-petalled, pale yellow, solitary amongst bracts in leaf axils; **leaves** stubby, fleshy, narrow with sharp spine tip.
Cayton, Sandsend.

Oraches *(Atriplex spp)* have separate male and female flowers on the same plant; fruits consist of two parallel triangular bracts enclosing seeds, giving an angular appearance to a mature plant. Often in large colonies.

COMMON ORACHE *Atriplex patula*
Variable annual up to 1m tall or semi-prostrate, sprawls on waste and arable land; stems ridged, often mealy or reddish. **Flowers** Aug-Sep, tiny, either male or female clustered on long spikes, spaced among leaves on upper stem; **leaves** sessile, pointed long oval on upper stem, toothed and ± triangular narrowing gradually into leaf stalk lower down.

SPEAR-LEAVED ORACHE *Atriplex prostrata*
Frequent sprawling annual on upper sandy shores; occasional inland in moist fertile fields and wasteland. Differs from common orache by a right-angled (not tapering) base to lower **leaves**; stems and flowers reddish.

GRASS-LEAVED ORACHE
Atriplex littoralis
Although not known on local shores, it is a prolific annual fringing the splash zone of some salt-treated roads eg. the eastern end of the A64 and the coast road north from *Whitby*. Erect branched stems up to 1m tall; tight **flower** clusters Jul-Aug; **leaves** long and narrow, grass-like, may be slightly toothed; **stems** often reddish.

FROSTED ORACHE *Atriplex laciniata*
Prostrate mealy annual, occasional on sandy shores near the tide-line; **leaves** silvery, fleshy; **flowers** Aug-Sep on stubby leafy spikes; sprawling stems reddish..

PINK FAMILY *CARYOPHYLLACEAE*

White or pink flowers, 4 or 5 sepals and petals, often notched or cleft to appear as 10. Leaf nodes often swollen.

RED CAMPION *Silene dioica*

Common colonial perennial in light shade with non-acidic soil on verges, woodside; hairy stems 30-90cm. **Flowers** Mar-Oct, 18-25mm, 5 deeply cleft petals, reddish, hairy, tubular calyx, male and female flowers on separate plants; **leaves** hairy, wide oval.

WHITE CAMPION *Silene latifolia*

An erect perennial or annual in small groups on field edge or verge; stems 30-100cm hairy, slightly sticky. **Flowers** May-Oct, 20-30mm with 5 deeply cleft white petals, hairy green calyx; male and female flowers on separate plants; **leaves** oval, hairy, in pairs.

Pale-flowered hybrids with intermediate features between white and red campion are frequent.

NIGHT-FLOWERING CATCHFLY *Silene noctiflora*

A southern sticky hairy annual, locally infrequent in calcareous cultivated ground; stems erect 15-60cm. **Flowers** Jul-Sep, 18mm diam, petals bifid, fragrant, white when open for pollination by night-flying insects; underside of curled up petals yellow or pink in daytime.

BLADDER CAMPION *Silene vulgaris*

Occasional on grassy banks, field edge or disturbed ground, especially on lime–rich soil. Almost hairless greyish perennial, stems 25-90cm. **Flowers** May-Aug, 18mm diam have 5 deeply cleft white petals, papery inflated calyx, striated lilac/bronze; **leaves** dull green, oval, in pairs on stems.

RAGGED ROBIN *Lychnis flos-cuculi*

SOAPWORT *Saponaria officinalis*

Colonial perennial occasional in marsh and streamside; erect stems 30-70cm. **Flowers** May-Aug, long-stalked 20-40mm across, 5 dark pink petals, each divided into 4 long twisted narrow lobes; **leaves** in pairs, hairless, narrow.

Showy garden perennial, long naturalised on road verges between *Seamer* and *Heslerton*. Fleshy, rather brittle, stems up to 1m tall were once used for soap-making. **Flowers** Jul-Sep, c.25mm across have long petal and calyx tubes; **leaves** oval, parallel-veined.

KNOTTED PEARLWORT *Sagina nodosa*
Short perennial infrequent on the edges of forest track-sides and moor edge. Flowering stems to 15cm grow from leafy ground mat. **Flowers** Jul-Sep, 5-15mm, bright white petals, longer than sepals, terminal on stems with spaced 'knots' or whorls of small **leaves,** all short linear with tiny end-point.

PROCUMBENT PEARLWORT *Sagina procumbens*
Moss-like low perennial common on paving and bare ground; flowering side shoots to 20cm grow from non-flowering central rosette. **Flowers** Apr-Sep, obscure, 4 (or 0) tiny white petals, 4 green sepals; **leaves** narrow, yellowish, short, form dense mat.

ANNUAL PEARLWORT *Sagina apetala*
Infrequent slender annual on sandy ground; resembles procumbent pearlwort but has spreading sepals and short-lived leaf rosette.

Chickweeds & **Stitchworts** *(stellarias)* have white flowers with 5 cleft petals, 5 sepals, 3 styles; *(myosoton 5 styles)*

COMMON CHICKWEED
Stellaria media
Common everywhere except on high moorland; sprawls over grass, waste, cultivated ground; annual with light green pointed oval **leaves**;slender round weak stems with single vertical lines of hairs between nodes. **Flowers** all year round, 5-8mm, have deeply cleft white petals, no longer than hairy sepals, <u>3-5 purple stamens.</u>

GREATER CHICKWEED
Stellaria neglecta
Early lowland plant of damp shady woodland, streamside, locally very sparse. Like common chickweed with single lines of hairs between nodes, but slightly larger, more upright to 90cm tall. **Flowers** Apr-Jul, 10-12mm, <u>10 stamens</u> often reddish; petals not shorter than sepals; fruit stalks ± erect.

LESSER CHICKWEED
Stellaria pallida
Small southern annual found infrequently in pavement cracks and sandy disturbed ground, often near the coast. Thin brittle stems have yellowish green **leaves**, small oval and fleshy. **Flowers** Mar-May, 3-6mm, 1-2 stamens, violet anthers but usually without petals.

Scarborough, Whitby

WATER CHICKWEED
Myosoton aquaticum
Lowland perennial with straggly stems to 1m tall, infrequent in sheltered damp habitats, wood edge and waterside. **Flowers** Jun-Oct, 2-15mm have 5 styles (stellarias 3) and bluish anthers; cleft petals longer than sepals; **leaves** often wavy-edged, stalked only on lower stems.

GREATER STITCHWORT
Stellaria holostea
Extensive on verges, woodside and grassy scrub, common in most areas away from high moors; colonial perennial with rough square stems 15-60cm. **Flowers** Apr-Jun, white 20-30mm with deeply notched petals longer than sepals; **leaves** bluish/green, paired, narrow, rough-edged, pointed.

LESSER STITCHWORT
Stellaria graminea
Widespread perennial in non-calcareous grassland; stems brittle, thin, square, shiny green, erect to 90cm, widely branched to form a spreading tangle. **Flowers** May-Aug, 5-18mm, later than greater stitchwort; anthers often red; 5 deeply cleft petals look like 10; **leaves** dark green, narrow, pointed.

BOG STITCHWORT
Stellaria uliginosa
Winter-green perennial common in acidic marshy ground, wet tracks and fens; low or prostrate, often secreted amongst taller vegetation; slender square hairless stems. **Flowers** May-Jun, small c.6mm with white deeply cleft petals shorter than exposed green sepals; **leaves** small oval, pointed, stalkless.

WOOD STITCHWORT
Stellaria nemorum
Northern perennial of damp, shady base-rich streamsides and hedgebanks; locally scarce. Pale green stems to 60cm, hairy all round; spreads by rhizomes. **Flowers** May-Aug, 15-20mm on slender glandular stalks, white petals much longer than pale-edged green sepals; **leaves** thin, broad oval.

MARSH STITCHWORT *Stellaria palustris* Marshland perennial with bluish foliage, always locally scarce, has not been seen for many years in its former known sites on banks of *Rivers Rye* and *Derwent*.

Mouse-ears are hairy with 5 styles except sea-mouse-ear 4 (chickweeds and stitchworts 3 styles).

COMMON MOUSE-EAR *Cerastium fontanum*

Tufted, dull green, sprawling perennial, common in rough grassland. **Flowers** Apr-Nov, 6-10 mm, petals slightly longer than sepals, deeply cleft; **leaves** hairy.

FIELD MOUSE-EAR *Cerastium arvense*

Patch-forming perennial in lime-rich grassland; erect stems to 30cm, **Flowers** Apr-Aug, 15-20mm, petals longer than glandular sepals; **leaves** narrow.

LITTLE MOUSE-EAR *Cerastium semidecandrum*

Occasional low annual on bare sandy soil; hairy with sticky glands; stems reddish. **Flowers** Apr-Oct, 5-7 mm, sepals and bracts with pale edge, 5 styles, 5 petals; hairy oval **leaves.**

STICKY MOUSE-EAR *Cerastium glomeratum*

Frequent annual, in small tussocks on bare or grassy ground. **Flowers** Apr-Oct, 5-8mm in clusters, shy to open; **leaves** sticky, hairy and yellowish green.

SNOW-IN-SUMMER *Cerastium tomentosum*

A frequent garden escape, also known as dusty miller from its white-felted mat-forming foliage. **Flowers** May-Aug, 10-20mm; looks greyish.

SEA MOUSE-EAR *Cerastium diffusum*

Uncommon low sprawling annual on sandy ground near the sea. **Flowers** Apr-Jul, tiny 3-6mm, 4 bifid petals shorter than green sepals, 4 styles; **leaves** sticky, hairy.

Spurreys have small 5-petalled flowers with un-notched petals, slender tangled stems, narrow linear sessile leaves.

LESSER SEA SPURREY
Spergularia marina

Occasionally both sea spurreys grow together.

GREATER SEA SPURREY
Spergularia media

Prostrate annual of saltmarshes, coastal sands and increasingly on the splash zone of salted roads. **Flowers** Apr-Sep, deep pink 6-8mm, sepals <4mm, stamens 2-7; flowers open about midday for a few hours; **leaves** short succulent form tangled mat.

Saltmarsh and dune slack perennial, sparse on tidal reaches of *River Esk*; much decreased as boating and building developments on the estuary have eliminated most of the saltmarsh. Rare inland. **Flowers** Jun-Sep, 8-12mm, sepals >4mm; usually 10 stamens; larger and paler than lesser sea spurrey; open for a few hours after midday; **leaves** fleshy, narrow, short-pointed.

CORN SPURREY *Spergula arvensis*

Frequent in arable fields on non-calcareous soils; sticky, hairy annual with weak tangled stems up to 30cm. **Flowers** Apr-Sep, 4-7mm on angled stems open in bright weather; sepals show between petals; **leaves** linear in loose whorls around stems.

SAND SPURREY *Spergularia rubra*

Short-lived creeping plant, uncommon on sandy heath and tracks *Rillington* to *Staxton*, also at *Lastingham* and rarely on forest rides. **Flowers** May-Sep, 3-5mm, soft mauve, open in sunlight; **leaves** short with awned tip.

ANNUAL KNAWEL
Scleranthus annuus
Sprawling annual or perennial to
25cm, infrequent on dry soils.
Flowers Jun-Aug c.4mm, no petals,
5 pale-edged sepals, 3 to 10
stamens; secreted in leaf axils;
leaves short, pointed.
Inconspicuous plant probably much
overlooked.

Sandworts have white or cream starry flowers with 5 un-notched petals.

THREE-NERVED SANDWORT *Moehringia trinervia*

Frequent slender
annual in open
woodland; downy lax
stems to 40cm.
Flowers Apr-Jul,
5-7mm on long stalks,
petals shorter than
intervening pointed
sepals.

leaves pointed oval with 3
distinct veins; light green
in sessile pairs on stems.

THYME-LEAVED SANDWORT *Arenaria serpyllifolia*

Low spreading or bushy hairy 3-20cm tall;
frequent on dry sandy ground, tracks, old
quarries and disturbed land. **Flowers** Apr-Sep,
3-5mm, petals shorter than exposed long

pointed
sepals; **leaves**
small, slightly
hairy, oval, in
sessile pairs
on branched
stems. Seeds
in numerous
small oval
capsules.

SEA SANDWORT *Honckenya peploides*

Succulent perennial creeps around on sandy
upper shores where infrequently covered by high
tides; can cover large patches. **Flowers** May-

Aug, 6-10mm
greenish white;
leaves yellow/
green, fleshy
triangular in
symmetrical
tiers on
succulent
prostrate
stems.

PINK *Dianthus sp*

Naturalised and flourishing on windswept cliffs at *Khyber Pass, Whitby* is a colourful perennial said to be a hybrid between clove and garden pinks; origin unknown.

PURSLANE FAMILY PORTULACACEAE

PINK PURSLANE *Claytonia sibirica*

C18th garden introduction often naturalised in damp wood and stream-sides. Stem 15-40cm hairless, erect, branched. **Flowers** Apr-Jul, 10-20mm, 5 pink notched petals, dark veined, 5 sepals, 5 stamens; **leaves** long-stalked basal, stalkless pairs clasp upper stems.

BLINKS *Montia fontana*

Unobtrusive ground-hugging small plant of water-logged non-calcareous soils; creeps to form low patches amongst mosses or grasses by springs, muddy tracks and streamsides. **Flowers** May-Oct, only 2-3mm, 5 tiny white petals; **leaves** small spoon-shaped in pairs.

SPRING BEAUTY *Claytonia perfoliata*

A short, hairless annual on well-drained, rather acid sandy ground. Locally known only on *Cayton* cliffs. **Flowers** Apr-Jul, c.4mm, 5 white petals; **leaves** fleshy, long-stalked from the base; a pair of sessile leaves encircles the upper stem.

DOCK FAMILY *POLYGONACEAE*

Herbs with simple, alternate leaves, wrapped at the stalk base by a silvery thin tubular sheath (ochrea); flowers small with 6 segments, inner 3 enlarge and harden to form triangular fruit, with or without red ovoid warts.

BROAD-LEAVED DOCK
Rumex obtusifolius
Common persistent perennial in fields, rough grassland. Robust erect branched stems to 1m. **Flowers** Jun-Oct, in whorls on upper stem; **leaves** on upper stem sessile, narrow; basal leaves stalked, oval, slightly wavy edged; **fruit** has <u>one enlarged reddish wart</u>, sepals toothed.

CURLED DOCK *Rumex crispus*
Frequent annual or short-lived perennial on wasteland, verges, arable and upper coastal sands. Branched stems up to 1m tall. **Flowers** Jun-Oct, in dense branched spikes; **leaves** narrow with distinctive curled edges; **fruit** pale, has large warts on 1 (rarely 3) smooth-edged sepals.

WATER DOCK
Rumex hydrolapathum
Large wetland perennial, locally rare; stems up to 2m tall with many flowering branches. **Flowers** Jul-Sep, in crowded whorls; **leaves** very large, up to 1m long and 16cm wide; **fruits** have large oval <u>warts on all 3</u> sepals. *Seamer.*

WOOD DOCK
Rumex sanguineus
Short-lived perennial frequent on shady hedgebanks, verges; stems to 1m tall, flowering branches upright. **Flowers** Jun-Sep, in spaced whorls on leafless upper stems; **leaves** at base, long oval, pointed; **fruit** has large <u>wart on one</u> smooth-edged sepal.

CLUSTERED DOCK
Rumex conglomeratus
Uncommon short-lived perennial in damp rough ground; stems to 60cm slightly zig-zag with wide spreading branches. **Flowers** Jun-Sep, in whorls on leafy upper stems; **leaves** at base long, pointed; **fruit** has large <u>warts on 3</u> smooth-edged sepals.

GOLDEN DOCK *R. maritimus*
Rare marshland annual up to 70cm. **Flowers** Jun-Sep, in crowded whorls; **leaves** narrow lanceolate, long tapering point; **fruit** has sepals with narrow, spreading teeth and <u>3 oblong warts</u>. Plant turns golden/ yellow in fruit.

© CHRIS WILSON

COMMON SORREL *Rumex acetosa*
Common perennial in more acidic soils, in rough grassland and on sea cliffs, often numerous. **Flowers** May-Aug, reddish in loose whorls, m and f on separate plants; **leaves** long arrow-shaped with prominent basal lobes, shiny; **fruit** roundish, small.

SHEEP'S SORREL *Rumex acetosella*

Patch-forming perennial on acidic ground, especially bare moorland where short erect stems and foliage turn red in late summer. **Flowers** May-Jul, reddish in loose whorls; **leaves** short lanceolate, with spreading pointed basal lobes; **fruit** tiny round red.

BLACK BINDWEED *Fallopia convolvulus*
Trailing or climbing annual, common in arable fields and disturbed ground; 1m long twining stems. **Flowers** Jun-Oct, small white, tinted pink and green, on long trailing spikes; **leaves** heart-shaped with silvery sheath at stalk base; **fruit** small black triangular nut.

JAPANESE KNOTWEED *Fallopia japonica*
A persistent shrubby garden escape occasionally forms thickets on verges or waste ground. Zig-zag reddish or bluish stems up to 2m. **Flowers** Aug-Oct, small white 5-petalled in short upright spikes; **leaves** broad oval, taper to end point.

REDSHANK or **REDLEG** *Persicaria maculosa*
Abundant and tiresome annual on cultivated and open ground, especially where damp. Tough patch-forming stems 70cm, reddish and swollen at nodes. **Flowers** Jun-Oct, tiny 5-petalled pink, packed in stubby stalked spikes; **leaves** lanceolate, green with dark blotching, fringed hairy ochrea.

PALE PERSICARIA *Persicaria lapathifolia*
Often grows with redshank but usually more bushy with green stems. **Flowers** Jun-Oct, greenish white; **leaves** with or without dark blotches; flower spike and larger oval leaves with shiny glands; ochrea scarcely fringed, hairless. Not as widespread as redshank.

COMMON BISTORT *Persicaria bistorta*
Infrequent perennial, forms large patches usually near water; hairless leafy stems erect 30-100cm. **Flowers** Jun-Aug, 4-5mm pink, 5-petalled with protruding stamens, packed into dense long terminal spikes; **leaves** on long, winged stalks, folded in bud, show creases when open.

AMPHIBIOUS BISTORT *Persicaria amphibia*
Occasional perennial in ponds and still water, also on almost dry rough grassy banks. **Flowers** Jul-Sep, are small pink, 5-petalled, in compact short spikes; **leaves** large oblong and floating in the water; the land form is shy to flower, has leaves smaller, more upright

WATER-PEPPER
Persicaria hydropiper
Spindly annual on muddy
or waterlogged ground,
usually on poor soil.
Nodding stems 25-75cm
have spaced small flower
clusters. **Flowers** Jul-Oct,
5 tiny green/white petals
with bright yellow glands;
leaves narrow lanceolate
with strong chilli-pepper
taste; ochrea red.

TASTELESS WATER-PEPPER *Persicaria mitis* is similar but more upright; leaves lack peppery taste; appears rarely in old peat cuttings.

KNOTGRASS
Polygonum spp.
Common low or prostrate
annuals on open disturbed
or trodden ground in fields,
seashore and gardens;
covers wide patches with
long wiry stems. **Flowers**
Jul-Oct, small pink, white
and green, part enclosed
by a ragged sheath giving a
"knotted" appearance.

COMMON KNOTGRASS
*Polygonum
aviculare*
Widespread either
upright or
spreading, with
sprawling stems to
1m. **Flowers** Jun-
Nov; **leaves** oval,
hairless; main stem
leaves much longer
than those on side
branches.

EQUAL-LEAVED KNOTGRASS
*Polygonum
arenastrum*
Differs from
common knotgrass
by leaves ± equal-
sized on the main
and side stems; a
smaller and more
prostrate plant;
frequent.

CORNFIELD KNOTGRASS
*Polygonum
rurivagum*
Lowland grass-like
annual of light
sandy calcareous,
disturbed land,
locally very
unusual, possibly
overlooked.
Flowers Jul-Nov,
reddish, single or in
pairs; **leaves** very
narrow, pointed.

ST JOHN'S-WORT FAMILY *CLUSIACEAE*

Perennial herbs and shrubs with opposite simple, smooth-edged leaves; flowers have 5 yellow petals, green sepals; type of stem, translucent leaf dots (holdup to the light) and/or black glands on flower parts help to determine species.

PERFORATE ST JOHN'S-WORT

Hypericum perforatum Common in drier, rather calcareous soils in rough grassland, open woods and waysides. Stem 30-90cm, round with 2 opposite raised ridges, often reddish; **leaves** have many translucent glands. **Flowers** Jun-Sep, 20mm, yellow with black glands on petal edges; sepals pointed.

HAIRY ST JOHN'S-WORT *Hypericum hirsutum*

Frequent in well-drained, non-acidic rough grassland, verges, glades. Stem 30-90cm, round, unridged, downy; **leaves** 2-5cm long, strongly veined, downy with translucent glands. **Flowers** Jun-Aug, 20mm pale yellow; sepals pointed, with stalked black glands.

SQUARE-STALKED ST JOHN'S-WORT
Hypericum tetrapterum

Frequent plant of damp meadows, stream and ditch sides. Stem 20-90cm square with 4 wings; **leaves** with translucent glands. **Flowers** Jun-Sep, 10mm, pale yellow; sepals pointed, narrow, no black glands.

PALE ST JOHN'S-WORT
Hypericum montanum

Rare lime-loving plant in disused limestone quarries or scrub. Stem stiff upright 40-80cm, round, slightly hairy; **leaves** hairless above, black dots on edge beneath; no translucent glands. **Flowers** Jul-Sep, pale yellow 10-15mm; sepals edged with stalked black glands.

IMPERFORATE ST JOHN'S-WORT *Hypericum maculatum* is rarely recorded in this area; a plant of damp shady places, also old quarries and rough grassland; stem 30-90cm, square without wings; **leaves** have few or no translucent glands. **Flowers** 20mm, deep yellow with black dots and streaks on petals Jun-Aug; **sepals** blunt.

MARSH ST JOHN'S-WORT *Hypericum elodes*
A low far-creeping coloniser on peaty or acidic, nutrient-poor wetland; very hairy foliage appears greyish; locally rare. **Flowers** Jun-Sep, 15mm across, grouped on short erect stems; **sepals** edged with red glands; **leaves** round to oval, covered with dense pale hairs.

TRAILING ST JOHN'S-WORT *Hypericum humifusum*
A low trailing plant on well-drained acidic soils; uncommon on heaths and tracks, frequent in rail ballast. **Stems** to 20cm, thin with 2 raised ridges. **Flowers** Jun-Sep, 10mm; glandular **sepals** unequal; **leaves** small narrow oval, usually with glands.

SLENDER ST JOHN'S-WORT *Hypericum pulchrum*
A short red-tinted plant on drier, acidic soils on heaths, open woods and moor edge. **Stem** 20-40cm round, often red. **Flowers** Jun-Aug, 15mm orange/yellow, red in bud; sepals and petals are edged with black glands; **leaves** small, blunt oval with cordate base and translucent dots.

TUTSAN *Hypericum androsaemum*
Small shrub, native in a few ancient woodlands, also escapes from gardens. Stem much branched, 2-ridged usually red. **Flowers** Jun-Aug, yellow 20mm, masses of long yellow stamens; sepals unequal, blunt; fruit large red berry turns black; **leaves** large, broad oval, aromatic when crushed.

ROSE-OF-SHARON *Hypericum calycinum* is a popular garden shrub which occasionally escapes to nearby hedgerows. Differs from tutsan by its single large flower and red anthers.

ROCK-ROSE FAMILY *CISTACEAE*

ROCK-ROSE *Helianthemum nummularium*

Spreading low shrublet, often extensive ground cover on short, dry calcareous grassland and stony outcrops. **Flowers** May-Sep, 20-30mm on downy stalks; petals yellow, thin and crinkly soon drop; **leaves** oval, green above, white woolly beneath, have inrolled margins, small stipules.

MALLOW FAMILY *MALVACEAE*

COMMON MALLOW *Malva sylvestris*

Colourful perennial on waste ground, waysides, often near habitation; robust bushy plant to 1m tall. **Flowers** Jun-Sep, 30-60mm, 5 petals pink/purple, dark-veined, notched; **fruit** resembles tiny cart-wheel in cup-shaped calyx; **leaves** large, tooth-edged with 5 or 7 shallow lobes, darker near the leaf stalk.

MUSK MALLOW *Malva moschata*

Occasional tall perennial, grows in colonies on well-drained soils in grassy wasteland, woodland edge and roadsides; tolerates light shade and disturbance; sometimes planted in gardens.

Flowers Jun-Aug, 30-60mm white or pale pink with lilac veins, petals slightly notched; loose flower clusters; stems hairy, upright to 80cm; **leaves** deeply cut into many narrow lobes.

DWARF MALLOW *Malva neglecta*

Infrequent low sprawling annual on waysides and bare ground. **Flowers** Jun-Sep, 10-20mm, in stem clusters or single; pale mauve with darker veins; **leaves** crinkled, almost round with shallow blunt lobes.

PERIWINKLE FAMILY *APOCYNACEAE*

GREATER PERIWINKLE *Vinca major*
Evergreen trailing shrublet; garden escape occasionally naturalised on banks and waste ground. **Flowers** Apr-Jul, single, 40-50mm, 5 petals blue/violet; **leaves** shiny, dark green, oval in pairs.
Lesser Periwinkle *Vinca minor* is similar but flowers smaller, 20-30mm.

VIOLET FAMILY *VIOLACEAE*

Violets (perennials) and pansies (annuals) have 5 colourful irregular petals, the bottom petal with a spur; a triangular capsule splits to release seeds. Sepal shape helps species identification. Both dog violet and sweet violet prefer shady sites; hairy violet favours open grassland; field and wild pansy grow in disturbed soils, usually on arable land; marsh violet requires wetland. Pansies have large leaf-like lobed stipules; violets have narrow undivided stipules.

FIELD PANSY *Viola arvensis*

Common tufted annual in many fields; upright leafy stems to 40cm. **Flowers** Apr-Oct and occasionally through the winter; 8-20mm; petals pale lemon/white with or without mauve tinting, spur similar; **sepals** pointed, show between or beyond petals; **leaves** pointed oval, slightly toothed; lobed stipules at base have large leaf-like end lobe.

WILD PANSY *Viola tricolor*

Strongly-coloured annual (rarely perennial) upright to 45cm. Locally scarce. **Flowers** Apr-Sep,15-25mm; petals variable, all purple or mixed yellow/cream/purple, spur similar; **sepals** pointed, equal to or shorter than petals; **leaves** narrow oval, slightly toothed; narrow lobed stipules.

MARSH VIOLET *Viola palustris*

Shy perennial, creeps amongst other vegetation in bogs, marshes and wet woodland on acidic soils. Not common and easily overlooked. **Flowers** Apr-Jul, only 10-15mm, pale mauve, streaked purple, short spur; **sepals** blunt; flowers and leaves long-stalked; leaves hairless, kidney-shaped.

COMMON DOG VIOLET *Viola riviniana*

Widespread low perennial in a range of habitats - woods, moors, grassy banks and gardens. **Flowers** Mar-May and sometimes late summer; 12-18mm, wider across than long; spur is ± curved, cream-coloured, stubby with a notched end; **sepals** pointed and large base lobe; **leaves** heart-shaped.

EARLY DOG VIOLET *Viola reichenbachiana*

Flowers a week or two earlier than dog violet and prefers a more shady habitat on lime-rich soil. **Flowers** early Mar-May, 12-18mm, outline long and narrow rectangle; scarcely fragrant; **spur** straight, slender, dark purple, end unnotched; **sepals** pointed and tiny base lobe; **leaves** cordate based and toothed, rather narrow.

HAIRY VIOLET *Viola hirta*

Low perennial occasional on calcareous short grassland, open rocky scrub or wood edge. Forms tight clumps as all shoots arise directly from the rootstock, no runners. **Flowers** Mar-May, light blue/violet; scentless spur is petal-coloured, often curved; **sepals** blunt; **leaves** pale green, narrow cordate; long spreading hairs on leaf blade and stalk.

SWEET VIOLET *Viola odorata*

Occasional on verges, hedgebanks and open woodland on base-rich soils. Long rooting stems create large spreads. **Flowers** Mar-May; fragrant, deep violet, white or tinted; sepals blunt; **leaves** crenate-edged, broad, glossy, cordate, enlarge in summer; downy hairs on stalks point down or absent.

YAM FAMILY DIOSCOREACEAE

BLACK BRYONY *Tamus communis*
Dioecious climber growing from a large underground tuber; widely
scattered by seed-eating birds; twines clockwise without tendrils
high into hedge or scrub, avoiding acid or very wet soils. **Flowers**
May-Jul,male 5mm stalked, female 4mm ± sessile, both yellow/
green; **leaves**
shiny green,
strongly veined,
heart-shaped,
finely pointed,
hairless; fruit a
poisonous red
berry on decay-
ing stems.

MARROW FAMIILY CUCURBITACEAE

WHITE BRYONY *Bryonia dioica*
Dioecious, tuberous perennial, climbs to over 4m with coiled tendrils;
stems bristly, angled. Locally rare, scrambles on hedgerows.
Flowers May-Sep, light green, 5-petalled, stalked male 12-18mm,
almost sessile
female 10-12
mm; **leaves**
coarse, large,
lobed, dull
green on curled
stalk. fruit a red
berry.

MIGNONETTE FAMILY RESEDACEAE

WELD *Reseda luteola*
Robust biennial
scattered in
small colonies
on waste
ground, old
quarries,
verges and field
edge, avoiding
acidic
moorland.
Hairless, ribbed
stems, stiffly
erect to 150cm.
Flowers Jun-
Sep, very small
4-5mm with <u>4
yellowish petals
and 4 sepals</u> on
long thin
spikes; **leaves**
long, narrow,
wavy-edged
and not lobed,
dark green.

MIGNONETTE *Reseda lutea*
Occasional on
well-drained
soils on verges,
railside, old
quarries and
field edge. A
biennial or
perennial, has
hairless, ribbed
stems erect or
spreading to
75cm.
Flowers Jun-
Sep, small
6-7mm with
<u>6 yellowish
narrow petals
and 6 sepals</u>, in
clusters on
broad spikes;
leaves pale
green, divided
into many
narrow lobes.

CABBAGE FAMILY BRASSICACEAE

A large group of plants including many edible species; all have 4 sepals, 4 petals and up to 6 stamens; species with similar flowers are easier to identify by distinctive fruits.

CHARLOCK Sinapis arvensis

Common on arable fields and waste; rough hairy annual erect to 1m. **Flowers** Apr-Nov, bright yellow, 15-20mm; **leaves** bristly, roughly-lobed and toothed; **pod** hairy, rather angular with short beak.

WILD RADISH Raphanus raphanistrum

Occasional in cultivated fields; bristly annual to 75cm. **Flowers** May-Oct, white, lemon or pale mauve, usually striated dark mauve; **leaves** deeply-lobed with large end-lobe; **pod** long-beaked.

OIL-SEED RAPE Brassica napus

Many fields turn yellow across the arable lands when oil seed rape flowers in early summer; stray plants often appear on nearby verges and waste. **Plant** erect to 1.5m; **flowers** bright yellow 18-30mm topped by young buds; **leaves** waxy grey/green, upper clasp the stem, lower leaves lobed; **pod** narrow tubular with beak, splits from the bottom upwards. Rape is grown for its oil and as a fodder crop.

BLACK MUSTARD Brassica nigra

Rare on waste ground or sea-cliff; bristly annual to 1m. **Flowers** Jun-Sep, 14-16mm with spreading sepals; **leaves** not clasping, simple on the stem, lobed and hairy lower down; **pods** slender, square, held erect close to the stem.

WHITE MUSTARD Sinapis alba

Game-cover crop has occasional escapes to the wild. Like charlock but paler flowers and all leaves stalked and lobed.

WILD CABBAGE *Brassica oleracae*

Robust perennial confined to coastal cliffs mainly northwards from Whitby. **Flowers** May-Aug, pale yellow 30-40mm; **leaves** large tough, crinkly-edged, bluish with red veins; **pod** long cylindrical, many seeded, beaked. Parent of several edible green vegetables.

HEDGE MUSTARD *Sisymbrium officinale*

Stiff, erect, hairy annual up to 1m tall; common on waysides and waste. **Flowers** May-Oct, pale yellow, only 3mm clustered at stem tops; **leaves** clasping on upper stem, lower leaves deeply lobed, large end segment; **pod** short, tubular, held close to the stem.

ANNUAL WALL ROCKET *Diplotaxis muralis*

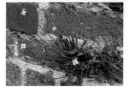

Infrequent casual on light sandy ground and walls; stems to 60cm. **Flowers** May-Sep, 10-15mm; **leaves** in basal rosette and on stem, deeply lobed.

EASTERN ROCKET *Sisymbrium orientale*

Straggly annual 25-90cm tall, rare on rough or rocky ground, walls. **Flowers** June onwards, 7mm pale yellow; **leaves** lobed in basal rosette, soon die back; stem leaves lanceolate; **pod** slender, up to 10cm long.

MARSH YELLOW-CRESS *Rorippa palustris*

Infrequent waterside
or wetland perennial.
Stems to 30cm;
flowers Jun-Sep,
2-3mm; **leaves**
toothed, often with
auricles; **pod** short
oval, curved.

CREEPING YELLOW-CRESS *Rorippa sylvestris*

Occasional in muddy
or flooded ground.
Flowers Jun-Sep,
4-6mm; square stems
spread to 60 cm;
leaves lobed and
unevenly toothed; **pod**
long, curve upwards.

WINTER-CRESS *Barbarea vulgaris*

Occasional in small groups on verges and
streamsides. **Flowers** May-Sep, 5-8mm, in dense
heads on stems up to 90cm; **leaves** deep shiny
green, pinnate with large end lobe.

TREACLE-MUSTARD *Erysimum cheiranthoides*

Rare annual on disturbed sandy soils; square stems
20-60cm have appressed 3-forked hairs; **flowers**
Jun-Sep, 5-7mm; **leaves,** lanceolate simple; **pods**
slender 4-angled.

WALLFLOWER *Erysimum cheiri*

Bushy, downy originator of many garden varieties; as a wilding grows in clumps on walls and old castles. **Flowers** Mar-Jun, large 20-30mm, fragrant, yellow; **leaves** simple, greyish, lanceolate with flattened forked hairs.

FLIXWEED *Descurainia sophia*

Locally uncommon on sandy soils; a tiny-flowered annual; stems to 1m tall have split hairs. **Flowers** May-Oct, only 3mm across, pale yellow, clustered at stem tops; **leaves** finely divided look fern-like; **pod** long thin erect.

FIELD PENNYCRESS *Thlapsi arvense*

Frequent on arable land, a sturdy annual erect to 60cm, named after its pod shape. **Flowers** May-Jul, white 4-6mm; **leaves** clasp stems, slightly toothed; **pod** flat, almost circular, with broad wing, notched at the top.

GARLIC-MUSTARD Alliaria petiolata

Common wayside perennial 30-120cm tall. **Flowers** Apr-Jul, 5-7mm, in stem-top cluster; **leaves** large, shiny, yellow/green tooth-edged, smell of garlic when bruised; **pod** long, angled.

COMMON WHITLOWGRASS *Erophila verna agg.*
Tiny early annual, scattered on walls and open dry
ground; stems to 10cm erect from leafy ground
rosette. **Flowers**
Jan-Apr, white
3-6mm, petals
deeply notched;
leaves all basal,
slightly toothed,
hairy; **pod** flat oval,
long-stalked.

SWINE-CRESS *Coronopus squamatus*
Small prostrate annual frequent in trampled muddy
areas; stems spreading to 30cm. **Flowers** May-Sep,
white 2-3mm; **leaves** deeply pinnate, greyish; **pod**
round with short beak and <u>wrinkled</u> surface.

LESSER SWINE-CRESS
Coronopus didymus is
pale green, infrequent on
disturbed ground. Has a
<u>smooth</u> round pod only
2mm, without beak.

HAIRY ROCK-CRESS *Arabis hirsuta*
Infrequent short greyish perennial on calcareous
ground; hairy, upright stems10-60cm. **Flowers** Jun-
Aug, white 3-4mm clustered; **leaves** hairy, clasping
on the stem, broader slightly toothed in ground
rosette; **pod** stiff, flattish, held erect.

THALE CRESS *Arabidopsis thaliana*
Frequent slender annual, grows in colonies on bare
ground; upright branched, thin stems to 30cm.
Flowers Mar-Oct, white, only 3mm in small clusters;
leaves few on stems; hairy, toothed on basal
rosette; **pod** long, angled up from stalks.

WAVY BITTERCRESS *Cardamine flexuosa*

Common small streamside plant; zig-zag slightly hairy stems to 50cm. **Flowers** Apr-Sep, white 2-3mm with 6 stamens; **leaves** pinnate, lobes narrower at stem top; **pod** narrow.

HAIRY BITTERCRESS *Cardamine hirsuta*

Abundant small annual on waste and disturbed ground; short stems usually straight and hairy. **Flowers** Feb-Nov and through mild winters; white 2-3mm with 4 stamens; **leaves** pinnate, hairy above, mostly in rosette; **pod** narrow.

LARGE BITTERCRESS *Cardamine amara*
Perennial 40-70cm tall, occasional in large groups on river banks and streamside; creeping stems produce erect flowering shoots. **Flowers** May-Jun, white 11-13mm with conspicuous violet anthers; **leaves** pinnate, light green, numerous; **pod** up to 4cm, angled away from stem.

WATERCRESS *Rorippa nasturtium-aquaticum*
Common salad perennial in lime-rich shallow streams; extensive hairless creeping hollow stems. **Flowers** May-Oct, white 4-6mm; **leaves** pinnate, stay green through winter; **pod** short, curved with 2 rows of seeds.

NARROW-FRUITED WATERCRESS *R.microphylla* is uncommon in more acid water; leaves turn brown in the winter and pod has a single row of seeds.

DAME'S VIOLET *Hesperis matronalis*

Prominent leafy garden escape on roadsides, grows to 90cm tall. **Flowers** May-Aug, white, mauve or purple, very fragrant, 15-20mm; **leaves** lanceolate, toothed, pointed and hairy; **pod** long, curved, cylindrical.

HONESTY *Lunaria annua*

Popular tall garden plant often naturalised on way-sides. **Flowers** Apr-Jun, purple or white, 28-30mm on stems to 1m; **leaves** heart-shaped, toothed; **pod** large (up to 7cm), flat.

CUCKOO FLOWER *Cardamine pratensis*

Common in damp grassland, ditch banks; also known as milkmaid or lady's smock; spreads by runners; erect stems to 60cm. **Flowers** Apr-Jun, pale lilac 10-18mm; **leaflets** narrow on upper stems, rounded lower down; **pod** straight, narrow.

CORALROOT *Cardamine bulbifera*

Early-flowering southern perennial, plentiful around *Scalby* church. Stems to 70cm grow from creeping rhizomes. **Flowers** Mar-Apr, 12-18mm in clusters; **leaves** simple or pinnate, lower leaflets slightly toothed. Purple **bulbils** form in leaf axils.

HOARY CRESS *Lepidium draba*

Patch-forming perennial, uncommon on waste and road verge. Branched stems 60-80 cm tall. **Flowers** May-Jul, greenish white 5-6mm, grouped at stem tops; **leaves** grey/green clasp stems; **pod** small, roundish with projecting style.

Whitby

FIELD PEPPERWORT *Lepidium campestre*

Rare casual on open gravel or sandy soils. Stems to 60cm, hairy, branches curved. **Flowers** May-Aug, 2.5mm; **leaves** greyish, clasping on stem, long-stalked and soon die back at base. **Pod** small oval, winged, style ± recessed.

HORSERADISH *Armoracia rusticana*

Former culinary herb grown to make a peppery sauce, frequently naturalised on verges; large leafy clumps up to 120cm tall. **Flowers** Aug-Sep, white 8-9mm but often flowering spikes checked by verge cutting; **leaves** prominent, shiny dark green, tongue-like, wavy-edged; **pod** small, roundish.

DITTANDER *Lepidium latifolium*

Unusual perennial on waste ground, mostly near the coast. Grows in large groups with stems to 1.5m tall. **Flowers** Jul-Aug, only 2-3mm in stem-top clusters; sepals white-edged; **leaves** lanceolate, unstalked on upper stems, large stalked strap-shaped lower down; **pod** small round, downy.

COMMON SCURVYGRASS *Cochlearia officinalis*

Low-growing, fleshy perennial, plentiful on coastal cliffs and upper shores, rare inland; small bushy plants form extensive colonies. **Flowers** Apr-Aug, white, fragrant, 8-15mm, numerous clusters on hairless stems; **leaves** almost round, some long-stalked, others stem-clasping; **pod** small globe.

DANISH SCURVYGRASS *Cochlearia danica*

Low-growing winter annual, has spread in recent decades to fringe the splash zone of winter-salted roads but not known on local sea cliffs. **Flowers** Jan-Sep, lilac or whitish, 4-5mm, bunched on short, often reddish stems; **leaves** ivy-leaf shaped or roundish, all stalked; **pod** small globe.

SHEPHERD'S-PURSE *Capsella bursa-pastoris*

Very common annual on fields, waysides; main stem 3-40cm usually branched. **Flowers** white 2-4mm, in bloom most of the year; **leaves** on stem narrow and clasping; in ground rosette almost simple to deeply lobed, with or without hairs; **pod** flat ± triangular, with notched upper edge.

SEA ROCKET *Cakile maritima*

Seashore low sprawling annual which appears infrequently on sandy beaches. **Flowers** Jun-Aug, pale mauve, 4 petalled; **leaves** fleshy, linear or lobed; **pod** small oval. *Sandsend, Cayton.*

WINTERGREEN FAMILY *PYROLACEAE*

Short perennials, patch-forming with creeping rhizomes in damp shady woodland; evergreen rather fleshy leaves; dainty small globe-like flowers pink/white, hang from short leafless erect stems.

COMMON WINTERGREEN
Pyrola minor
Grows in a few small, scattered groups in deciduous woods and forested old woodland. Flowering stems 10-30cm carry 5-petalled bell **flowers** Jun-Aug, c.6mm with style 1-2mm almost concealed by petals; **leaves** oval, crenate-edged.
Troutsdale, Reasty, Cropton, Newtondale.

INTERMEDIATE WINTERGREEN
Pyrola media
Like common wintergreen, in similar habitats but locally very rare. Flowering stems 15-30cm with bell flowers; style 5mm long projects below petals. **Leaves** almost circular. Native of Scottish pinewoods, its 2 known local sites are the most southerly in UK.
Reasty

SEDGE FAMILY *CYPERACEAE*

Moorland and wetland showy sedges in bogs and shallow pools, creeping and patch-forming. Stems up to 60cm tall, slightly triangular, have waving tufts of white fruiting heads; leaves grass-like.

COMMON COTTONGRASS
Eriophorum angustifolium
Widespread in wet acidic ground May-Jul; white fluffy fruiting heads from a distance resemble a light covering of snow. Stems smooth and 3-sided only at the top, carry clusters of up to 7 stalked and nodding spikes; leaves long, usually reddish, 3-5mm wide with long triangular tip and short ligule.

HARE'S-TAIL COTTONGRASS
E.vaginatum
Common on wet acid peat, especially blanket bogs; forms tussocks Apr-May; leaves only 1mm wide, triangular, have strongly inflated sheath; flowering stems to 60cm, 3-sided at the top, each with a single spike.

BROAD-LEAVED COTTONGRASS *E. latifolium*
Infrequent, restricted to wet calcareous ground May-Jul; stems 3-sided throughout with up to 12 stalked spikes; leaves 3-8mm wide with short triangular tip and no ligule.

HEATH FAMILY *ERICACEAE*

HEATHER or LING   *Calluna vulgaris*

Semi-woodland undershrub, managed on acidic upland to maintain habitat for grouse and hill sheep flocks. **Flowers** Aug-Sep, pink/purple (rarely white), 4 petals joined to form a bell 3-4mm; several on short spikes; **leaves** tiny linear, pressed to the stem in vertical rows; **fruit** a 2mm capsule.

CROSS-LEAVED HEATH   *Erica tetralix*

A common and extensive greyish downy shrublet on damp moorland. **Flowers** Jun-Oct, rose-pink 6-7mm bell-shaped, hang in a cluster at the stem tip; **leaves** short greyish linear in whorls of 4, leaf margins turned inwards on underside; glandular hairs on sepals and leaves.

BELL HEATHER   *Erica cinerea*

Frequent short shrublet on drier moorland and free-draining upland banks with thin, acidic soils. **Flowers** Jul-Sep, strong purple 4-6mm, several on short leafy twigs; **leaves** dark green, short linear in close whorls of 3 up stems; edges inrolled underneath.

ST DABEOC'S HEATH   *Daboecia cantabrica*

Recent discovery on moorland north of *Beadlam* is an Irish heath, unknown elsewhere in northern England. A few plants are mingled with crowberry and bell heather on a steep north-facing bank. **Flowers** Jun-Sep, large 8-14mm; **leaves** larger than above heaths, green above, whitish below, margins inrolled.

BILBERRY *Vaccinium myrtillus*
Common and extensive, hairless, deciduous shrub on drier moorland and in acid woodland; stems green ±
square. **Flowers** Apr-Jun, 4-6mm, bell-shaped with 5 tiny teeth; **leaves** light green, oval, finely toothed;
fruits Jul-Aug, edible black berry with pale bloom.

COWBERRY *Vaccinium vitis-idaea*
Spreading evergreen shrublet, occasional on moors and in acidic
woodland; stems upright to 30cm. **Flowers** Jun-Aug, pale pink, 4 joined
pointed petals form small bell 5-8mm; **leaves** leathery, slightly notched at
apex, dark, shiny, green above, pale and gland-dotted beneath; **fruit** edible red berry.

CRANBERRY *Vaccinium oxycoccos*
Slender trailing ground-hugging evergreen, scattered in bogs, often
secreted amongst sphagnum moss. **Flowers** Jun-Jul, on long slender
stalks, have 4 bright pink curled-back petals surrounding a projecting
column of yellow stamens 6-10mm; **leaves** tiny oval, spaced on thread-like stems; **fruit** edible roundish bronze/red berry.

BOG-ROSEMARY *Andromeda polifolia*
Dwarf shrub locally known only on wet peat at *May Moss*
north of *Saltergate*. Stems hairless, evergreen, upright to
30cm. **Flowers** Apr-Sep, pale pink bell-shape 5-8mm,
hang singly on long pink stalks; **leaves** narrow with
inrolled edges, glossy grey/green above, pale beneath;
fruit a dry capsule.

RHODODENDRON *Rhododendron ponticum*
An invasive, large, colourful, evergreen shrub/small tree which creates dense cover and eliminates native woodland vegetation; widely planted during C19th, efforts are now made to eradicate it from many woods. **Flowers** May-Jun, 5-petalled, mauve/pink, several form large clustered heads; **leaves** dark green, leathery, strap-shaped, up to 12cm long.

CROWBERRY FAMILY EMPETRACEAE

CROWBERRY *Empetrum nigrum*

Low spreading evergreen bush at the south-eastern limit of its UK range; frequent patches on moorland, especially after burning. Stems reddish, tough. **Flowers** May-Jun, tiny 1-2mm, dioecious, 6 petals; protruding stamens on male plants; **leaves** small linear, tightly inrolled edges on underside; **fruit** shiny small black berries.

SUNDEW FAMILY DROSERACEAE

ROUND-LEAVED SUNDEW *Drosera rotundifolia*

Insectivorous low perennial, frequent in acid peat on wet moorland; sticky glandular hairs trap insects to augment low nitrate intake in its bog habitat. **Flowers** Jun-Aug, on 10-20cm slender, upright stems; small, white 5-petalled, open in bright light; **leaves** long-stalked in a ground rosette; round blades have glandular sticky hairs which curve inwards to trap prey.

PRIMROSE FAMILY *PRIMULACEAE*

Flowers with 5 similar petals joined into tube at base; leaves without stipules, usually in ground rosette.

PRIMROSE *Primula vulgaris*
Frequent perennial on wood-edge and grassy banks. **Flowers** Mar-May, fragrant, 20-40mm pale yellow, deep yellow centre; single on hairy stalks up to 12cm; **leaves** all basal, blades crinkly, taper into stalk.

FALSE OXLIP
Primula
x polyantha
Intermediate features on a range of hybrids.

COWSLIP *Primula veris*
Common perennial in non-acid grassland, road verges. **Flowers** Apr-May, fragrant, deep yellow 8-15mm, with long tube and pale hairy calyx, hang to one side; **leaves** crinkly, blades narrow abruptly into stalks.

BIRD'S-EYE PRIMROSE *Primula farinosa*

CHICKWEED-WINTERGREEN *Trientalis europaea*

Confined to few sites in northern England, rare perennial in damp pasture. **Flowers** May-Jun, 7-15mm, soft mauve/pink with yellow centre, several in open head on short stalks; **leaves** form ground rosette, blades green above, mealy white beneath.

Elusive perennial on acidic, humus-rich upland soils, at its southern UK limit; often numerous beneath bracken or after felling. Slender stems 10-20cm with one or two starry **flowers** Jun-Aug, 15-18mm diam with 5-9 petals; each stem has whorl of 5-8 pointed oval **leaves.**

DOTTED LOOSESTRIFE *Lysimachia punctata*
Evergreen perennial often naturalised from gardens.
Stems to 1m. **Flowers** Jun-Aug, almost stalkless, 10-
16mm, yellow with dark centre, 5 petals edged with
glandular hairs; sepals all
green; **leaves** large pointed,
short stalked, 3 or 4 in
whorls.

TUFTED LOOSESTRIFE *Lysimachia thyrsiflora*
Hairless perennial rare in England, has a
stronghold in Scotland. Stems to 70cm. **Flowers** in
clusters, Jun-Jul, only 5mm, petals narrow; **leaves**
and petals with black
glandular dots. On the
shores of *Lake Gormire*.

YELLOW LOOSESTRIFE   *Lysimachia vulgaris*   A lowland plant of fen and riverside up to 1.5m tall, locally rare.
Flowers Jul-Aug, single on short stalks, 8-15mm, petals bright yellow without hairs; sepals green, edged orange;
leaves almost stalkless are dotted with black glands.

WATER-VIOLET *Hottonia palustris*
Rare aquatic in ditches with non-eutrophic water; erect
flower stems to 40cm emerge May-Jun. **Flowers** 25mm
mauve, yellow centre, stalked in whorls; **leaves** in stem
whorls finely divided, submerged and floating.

SEA MILKWORT *Glaux maritima*
Low creeping perennial, mat-forming on seashores
and saltmarsh; **leaves** small fleshy, numerous on
stems prostrate or upright to 30cm. **Flowers** May-
Sep, small 5-lobed in leaf axils .

YELLOW PIMPERNEL *Lysimachia nemorum*
Common creeping, hairless low perennial, covers large

patches in damp woodland edge and light shade. **Flowers** May-Aug, c.10mm, star-like, face skywards, solitary on long slender stalks; **leaves** evergreen, pointed oval in pairs.

CREEPING JENNY *Lysimachia nummularia*
Infrequent low carpeting perennial in damp shady woodland

and streamsides. **Flowers** Jun-Aug, bell-shaped, 15mm on short stalks, petals with yellow glands especially on edges; **leaves** almost round, dotted with black glands.

BOG PIMPERNEL *Anagallis tenella*

Creeping perennial forms extensive mats in less acid bogs and fens. **Flowers** May-Sep, delicate pale pink bell-shaped, 6-10mm, on long thin stalks; **leaves** small roundish in pairs on prostrate rooting stems.

SCARLET PIMPERNEL *Anagallis arvensis*
Colourful small annual, occasional on cultivated or open ground; hairless square stems upright or creeping to 30cm. **Flowers** May-Oct, starry c.12mm across, long- stalked; petals fringed with tiny hairs, normally brick-red; unusual colour forms appear rarely. **Leaves** oval pointed in pairs.

CURRANT FAMILY GROSSULARIACEAE

Leafy shrubs with bunches of small pink/green flowers with 5 petals late Mar-May; later produce juicy-berried fruits eaten by humans and wildlife.

GOOSEBERRY Ribes uva-crispa

Branched deciduous hairy shrub to 1m tall with strongly spined twigs; cultivated for its edible fruit; frequent in hedgerows, scrub and woodside. **Flowers** Mar-May, 6-12mm, in stalked sprays; petals yellow/red, soon reflexed; **leaves** toothed, short-stalked; **fruit** green hairy berry.

BLACK CURRANT Ribes nigrum

Infrequent deciduous shrub 1-2m in damp ground or streamside, cultivated for its edible fruit. **Flowers** Apr-May, 8mm purple/greeen, hang in small sprays; **leaves** large, 3-5 lobed, hairless, smell fruity; **fruit** juicy, black, shiny berry.

RED CURRANT Ribes rubrum

Deciduous shrub to 2m tall, occasional in open woods, hedges, scrub; planted in gardens for its fruit. **Flowers** Apr-May, 4-6mm, cream, edged red, hang in small sprays; **leaves** 3-5 lobed, shiny beneath; not fragrant; **fruit** juicy red berry.

MOUNTAIN CURRANT Ribes alpinum

Deciduous shrub widely branched up to 2m; rare native on limestone. **Flowers** Apr-May, only 2-3mm, all yellow/green in upright sprays, male and female on separate plants; **leaves** small, deeply toothed; **fruit** shiny red berries on erect sprays. *Rievaulx*

STONECROP FAMILY *CRASSULACEAE*

A family of succulents with small, undivided, fleshy leaves.

BITING STONECROP *Sedum acre*

NEW ZEALAND PIGMYWEED *Crassula helmsii*

Widespread, creeping ground cover. Also called wall pepper from its tangy-tasting leaves; covers walls, dry bare ground, rocky places. **Flowers** Jun-Jul, bright yellow, 5-petalled star-like 10-14mm; **leaves** small oval fleshy on tangled mat of prostrate stems.

Introduced in 1927, an aggressive evergreen perennial which has spread rapidly into ponds and ditches; forms dense cover suffocating other plants. **Flowers** Jun-Aug, tiny 1-2mm, whitish 4-petalled in leaf axils; **leaves** small linear on reddish stems.

REFLEXED STONECROP *Sedum rupestre*

WHITE STONECROP *Sedum album*

Introduced from southern Europe for its edible leaves; infrequently naturalised on walls and rocks. **Flowers** Jun-Aug, c.15mm, yellow, 6 petals; **leaves** fleshy, spreading or drooping on creeping and upright stems 10-30cm.

Occasional low perennial, dense creeping and erect stems on walls, rocks and broken concrete. **Flowers** Jun-Aug, 6-9mm, white pink-tinted, 5-petals; **leaves** small fleshy oval, shiny green.

SAXIFRAGE FAMILY   *SAXIFRAGACEAE*

GRASS-OF-PARNASSUS   *Parnassia palustris*

A beautiful, though infrequent, perennial of nutrient-rich flushes, fen and marsh, numerous on coastal cliffs; stems hairless, upright 10-30cm. **Flowers** Jul-Sep, 15-30mm, solitary with green centre and golden stamens, 5 rounded white petals, green-veined; **leaves** several cordate long-stalked, grow from the ground, a single stalkless leaf clasps each flower stem.

MEADOW SAXIFRAGE   *Saxifraga granulata*
Infrequent perennial on lime-rich grass-land or wood edge; stems up to 50cm hairy sticky, branched, with bulbils at the base. **Flowers** Apr-Jun, 18-30mm with 5 spaced open white petals; **leaves** kidney-shaped with shallow, rounded lobes.

RUE-LEAVED SAXIFRAGE
Saxifraga tridactylites
Tiny winter annual with sticky glandular hairy stems up to 10cm, often reddish; occasional on limestone walling or stony ground. **Flowers** Apr-May, bell-shaped, white 4-6mm; **leaves** only 1cm, palmate with 3-5 lobes, often reddish, stalked.

GOLDEN SAXIFRAGE *Chrysosplenium spp*

Two closely allied species, common by streams and springs, often extensive carpeting on marshy ground; occasionally they grow together. Both have tiny golden flowers 3-5mm, with 4 sepals and bracts but no petals Feb-Jul.

Opposite-leaved golden saxifrage *C.oppositifolium* is square-stemmed. It has opposite pairs of stalked small wedge-shaped **leaves**, wavy-edged. **Flowers** numerous on prostrate stems; more frequent than the alternate-leaved species.

Alternate-leaved golden saxifrage *C.alternifolium* is triangular-stemmed; **leaves** are alternate with blades more evenly crenated, larger and sparsely hairy. **Flowers** are slightly larger and brighter; prefers a more limey habitat. Not common.

PURPLE LOOSESTRIFE FAMILY *LYTHRACEAE*

PURPLE LOOSESTRIFE *Lythrum salicaria*
Scarce, showy, waterside perennial; square stems to 120cm tall have dense terminal spikes. **Flowers** Jun-Aug, 10-15mm, with narrow, pointed petals and dark stamens; leaves lanceolate, mostly in stem whorls.

WATER-PURSLANE *Lythrum portula*
Easily overlooked small creeping annual in upland pools or mud; hairless rooting stems often reddish. **Flowers** Jun-Sep, tiny 1mm, single at base of small spoon-shaped leaves.

ROSE FAMILY ROSACEAE

DOG ROSE *Rosa canina* group includes several closely-related species which hybridise. Most frequent here are:

Northern dog rose *R caesia*. Common, clambering in hedgerows and scrub.
Flowers Jun-Jul, pink 5cm, on short stalks with large leafy bracts; stems strong
arching, often reddish with robust hooked prickles; **leaflets** green above, caesious
(blue/green) beneath; **hips** red egg-shaped on short stalks, sepals erect.

Dog rose *R.canina* A tall scrambler frequent in hedgerows. **Flowers** Jun-Jul, up to
6cm, pale pink or white on smooth stalks; stems arching with stout hooked prickles;
leaflets ± glabrous, shiny; **hips** red long stalked; sepals lobed, reflexed, soon fall off.

DOWNY ROSES have slightly fragrant glands, mostly straight prickles and bristly hips.

Sherard's downy rose *R. sherardii* Occasional in scrub and wood edge. **Flowers**
Jun-Jul, deep pink, 3.5cm, on glandular stalks; stems with slender slightly curved
prickles; **leaflets** softly hairy, greyish, glandular; **hips** with spreading fringed sepals.

Soft downy rose *R.mollis* Occasional suckering shrub more frequent further north.
Flowers Jun-Jul, deep pink 4.5cm diam; stem reddish with slender straight prickles;
leaflets large, greyish softly hairy, glandular; **hips** glandular, short-stalked, sepals
erect and persistent, not fringed.

SWEET BRIAR *Rosa rubiginosa*   Scarce throughout UK, locally rare in limestone scrub. **Flowers** bright pink 3-
4cm Jun-Jul; **stems** covered with
stout curved and slender straight
prickles and stalked sticky glands;
leaflets have
brownish
glands
beneath; **hips**
red, persist,
sepals slightly
fringed; leaflets
and hips smell
of apples.

FIELD ROSE *R. arvensis*

Lowland species uncommon at its northern UK limit; long trailing stems with narrow hooked prickles. **Flowers** Jun-Aug, soon after dog rose; white 3-5cm; styles joined in a projecting column prominent above surrounding stamens; **leaflets** ± hairless, thin pale, stalks glandular; **hip** small oval, red; small sepals soon fall.

BURNET ROSE *R. pimpinellifolia*

Infrequent in old mixed hedgerows and scrub on lime-rich soil; suckers widely. **Flowers** May-Jul, creamy white 2-4cm; stems are covered with straight prickles and bristles; **leaflets** small, roundish, often bronze; **hips** large black, shiny, round, sepals persist.

MANY-FLOWERED ROSE *R. multiflora*
Dense climbing garden escape occasionally naturalised in hedgerows. **Flowers** Jun-Aug, only 2-3cm in clusters; stems usually prickly, much branched; **leaflets** small, pale, on glandular prickly stalks; **hips** small, red with projecting style; short triangular sepals fall early.

JAPANESE ROSE *R.rugosa*

19th introduction planted in parks and gardens, often naturalised in large thickets, particularly along the coast. **Flowers** Jun-Jul, 6-8cm, deep pink; stems have dense hairs and prickles; **leaves** rough, dark green, deeply veined, downy grey beneath; **hips** large, erect sepals.

BRAMBLE *Rubus fruticosus agg.*

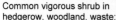

Common vigorous shrub in hedgerow, woodland, waste; spreads extensively by long rooting branches. Varied with over 400 microspecies. **Flowers** May-Nov, white or pink, 20-30mm; **leaves** 3 or 5 lobed, roughly toothed; hooked prickles on clambering stems; **fruit** edible shiny bramble or blackberry; <u>many</u> packed juicy <u>segments.</u>

DEWBERRY *Rubus caesius*

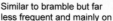

Similar to bramble but far less frequent and mainly on lime-rich soils; stems glaucous, rarely reach 1m high, have smaller, fewer spines than bramble. **Flowers** Jun-Sep, white 15-25mm; **leaves** 3-lobed with soft prickles; **fruit** looks grey with waxy bloom on its <u>few segments</u>; edible but tasteless.

RASPBERRY *Rubus idaeus*

Forms open thickets in rough wooded areas and scrub. Quite frequent; dispersed by birds and dumping of garden rubbish. Suckers give rise to 1.5m tall stems with slender prickles. **Flowers** May-Aug, c.10mm, drab white, 5 petals soon fall; leaves pinnate, large leaflets white tomentose beneath; **fruit** has red, downy, edible, juicy segments. Widely cultivated.

STONE BRAMBLE *Rubus saxatilis*

Northern upland small shrub, very scarce. Grows in rocky semi-shade on non-acidic soils. **Flowers** Jun-Aug, 8-15mm, with green sepals showing between 5 dull white, narrow, erect petals; **leaves** 3-lobed, downy beneath; stems spread to 40cm and have few or no weak prickles; fruit is sparse, red when ripe, only 1-5 red segments.

CLOUDBERRY *Rubus chamaemorus*

An upland dioecious perennial of peat moorland, has an isolated outpost on *May Moss* north of *Saltergate*. **Leaves** a single blade, scallop-edged. **Flowers** rarely, Jun-Aug, 15-25mm; **fruit** large, segments turn orange.

© *CHRIS WILSON*

CHINESE BRAMBLE *Rubus tricolor*

Vigorous trailing perennial, first cultivated in UK in 1908 as amenity ground cover, increasingly naturalised on waste and scrubland. Rooting stems, several metres long, have dense brown bristles.

Leaves simple, large, shiny green, 3-5 shallow lobes. **Flowers** white 20-25mm; fruit red, but local plants not known to flower. *Cawthorn.*

WILD CHERRY or GEAN *Prunus avium*

Small tree with peeling bark, widespread in hedgerows and light woodland; suckers create extensive cherry colonies. **Flowers** Mar-May, white, 15-25mm in bunches; **leaves** green or bronze, with 2 small reddish pimples or glands where stalk and blade join; **fruit** long- stalked; small ripe cherries soon eaten by birds.

BLACKTHORN *Prunus spinosa*

Common shrub or small tree in hedge and scrub throughout except on high moorland; rooting suckers create impenetrable thickets with dark grey, spiny branches. **Flowers** white 8-15mm open by late March, a week or two before the green leaves unfold; **leaves** small oval, pointed and neatly- toothed; **fruit** small dark purple plum; larger and intermediate fruits produced on bullace (sloe), a closely related shrub, and hybrids.

CHERRY PLUM *Prunus cerasifera*

Uncommon, early-flowering small tree or hedgerow shrub. Young twigs glossy green, spine-less. **Flowers** Feb-Apr, solitary, white c.20mm; **leaves** pale, glossy green, appear with the flowers; **fruit** globular, yellow or red but some trees rarely fruit.

WILD PLUM *Prunus domestica*
Variable small tree or shrub occasional in hedgerows and scrub, generally assumed to be relics from gardens and abandoned orchards, possibly dispersed by birds. **Flowers** Apr-May, white 15-25mm, with the leaves; twigs sometimes thorny, downy when young. The diverse origins of these plants show in a variety of purple/black and green fruits and includes sloes, green and golden gages, plums and damsons.

BIRD CHERRY *Prunus padus*

Northern tree up to 15m tall, frequent near streams. **Flowers** May-Jun, small, fragrant, clustered to form 'candles' 10-16cm long; **leaves** thin, pointed, oval, pale green with 2 small red stalk glands like wild cherry; **fruits** small, astringent but usually eaten by birds before maturing to black berries.

ROWAN or MOUNTAIN ASH *Sorbus aucuparia*

Small tree up to 20m, frequent in dale heads and upland woods on non-calcareous soils. **Flowers** May-Jun, cream, 5-petalled, aromatic, form large domed bunches; **leaves** pinnate with toothed leaflets; orange/red berries.

HAWTHORN *Cratageus monogyna*

Common tree and hedge plant absent only from open moor and extreme wetland. Also known as quickset or whitethorn, it was extensively planted to create stock-proof hedges when open fields were enclosed; can grow to a small gnarled tree. **Flowers** Apr-Jun, white or pink 8-15mm in small leafy bunches, noted for strong 'May blossom' fragrance; **leaves** deeply indented; **fruits** are round red haws.

CRAB APPLE *Malus sylvestris*

Small tree with angular branches and thorny twigs showing wrinkled leaf scars. Quite frequent in old hedgerows on lower ground. **Flowers** Apr-May, 30-40mm in small clusters; **leaves** oval, pointed and toothed; hairless when mature - unlike leaves on cultivated apple trees which remain downy; **fruits** small, yellowish apples which remain on the tree and ground below often until spring.

AGRIMONY

Common upright perennial to 1m tall in groups on waysides, grassy banks; **Flowers** Jun-Sep, 5-petalled, yellow 5-7mm, sessile on upper stems; **leaves** long pinnate with toothed leaflets, alternate large and small; **fruit** small bell-shaped with a ring of hooked hairs; the two species hybridise.

COMMON AGRIMONY

Agrimonia eupatoria has spreading or downward-pointing fruit hairs when ripe; few, scarcely-fragrant, glands on stem & leaves.

FRAGRANT AGRIMONY

Agrimonia procera is far less frequent; a larger and more fragrant plant with many glandular lemon-scented hairs; its fruit has backward-pointing

and spreading hooked hairs when ripe.

GREAT BURNET *Sanguisorba officinalis*

Occasional perennial in unimproved neutral grassland, meadows, verges and river banks. Waving stems c.1m tall are topped with single flower-heads. **Flowers** Jun-Sep, tiny, dark red, packed into oblong heads 1-2cm long; **leaves** pinnate with up to 7 pairs of oval, toothed, cordate-based leaflets.

SALAD BURNET *Sanguisorba minor*

Frequent on lime-rich short grassland. Solitary globe-shaped flower-heads top branched stems up to 50cm. **Flowers** May-Aug, tiny, with red styles and yellow stamens, packed into dense globular flowerheads; **leaves** pinnate, c.12 pairs of roundish toothed leaflets, smell of cucumber if crushed.

WATER AVENS *Geum rivale*

WOOD AVENS *Geum urbanum*

Perennial herb, spreads widely in damp semi-shade by streams, in woods and wet grassland. Nodding, often reddish, stems up to 50cm. **Flowers** Apr-Sep, hang down, bell-shaped 10-18mm; hairy sepals surround 5 orange/pink petals; **leaves** long-stalked with a single large end leaflet; smaller leaves on stems; **fruit** oval bur with hooked hairs.

HYBRID AVENS *G. x intermedium* with a range of intermediate features often occurs where the two species both grow nearby.

Common perennial of hedge banks and woodside, also known as herb bennet. Hairy branched stems up to 70cm. **Flowers** May-Nov, star-like, 8-15mm; pointed, green sepals show between 5 (6) yellow petals; **leaves** long-stalked with 3-lobed end leaflet; smaller toothed stem leaves; **fruit** a round bur with hooked hairs.

BARREN STRAWBERRY *Potentilla sterilis*

WILD STRAWBERRY *Fragaria vesca*

Early-flowering low perennial, common on dry banks and scrub. Sprawling stems up to 15cm with short runners. **Flowers** Feb-May, 10-15mm have pointed green sepals which show between 5 spaced, notched, white petals; **leaves** trifoliate, hairy, greyish, toothed with short end-point.

Frequent perennial on woodside, road and rail banks with dry stony soils. Plants erect to 20cm, spread widely by rooting runners. **Flowers** Apr-Jul, 12-18mm, white, petals conceal sepals beneath; **leaves** shiny green, trifoliate, on long stalks, have obvious end-point to leaflets; **fruit** sweet juicy, edible.

MEADOWSWEET *Filipendula ulmaria*
Common on less acidic wet soils; spreads widely in damp areas. Stems branched sturdy reddish up to 1m tall. **Flowers** 5 petalled cream/white 5-10mm in large frothy clusters, almond-scented Jun-Sep; **leaves** large pinnate up to 60cm long, pale beneath; three-lobed end leaflet, 2-5 pairs side leaflets alternate large and tiny, all unevenly toothed; **fruits** join in twisted spiral.

DROPWORT *Filipendula vulgaris*
Beautiful though scarce perennial on lime-rich grassland. Reddish stems 10-50cm have open flower sprays. **Flowers** 5 or 6-petalled cream 10-20mm, buds pink May-Aug. **leaves** mainly basal with numerous toothed large and tiny leaflets, all darkish green.

LADY'S MANTLE *Alchemilla spp*
Aggregate of several northern species of which 3 occur locally. *A. xanthochlora,* the most frequent, has few or no hairs on upper leaf surface but is hairy elsewhere. *A. glabra* has hairless leaves and appressed soft hairy stems. *A. vestita* has spreading hairs on stems and both leaf surfaces. All are spreading low perennials in rough grassy places, pathsides, on non-acidic soil. **Flowers** 3-5mm, 2 rings of yellow/green sepals (no petals), bunched in small erect sprays Jun-Aug; **leaves** give the plant its name from their resemblance to a cape; neatly lobed, toothed and pleated when young.

PARSLEY PIERT *Aphanes arvensis*
Tiny, ground-hugging inconspicuous annual. common on bare grassland, dry and disturbed soils. **Flowers** less than 2mm, secreted in leaf axils; 4 yellow/green sepals (no petals) Apr-Oct; **leaves** small fan-shaped, fringed; **Slender parsley piert** *A.australis* is a smaller more lowland plant, prefers acid soils, locally rare.

BRIDEWORT *Spiraea salicifolia*
Deciduous suckering shrub, occasional garden escape in thickets. **Flowers** bright pink in dense short spikes on long willowy stems Jun-Aug; **leaves** greyish, slightly toothed.

TORMENTIL *Potentilla erecta*
Short creeping perennial, often sheep-nibbled to form

flowering mat; abundant on moorland heath and acidic waysides, woods. **Flowers** Jun-Sep, yellow.8-12mm, 4 petals create 'square' flower; **leaves** dark green, shiny, silky white below, clasp the main stem with 3 leaflets and 2 leaf-like stipules.

CREEPING CINQUEFOIL *Potentilla reptans*
Extensive low perennial, frequent on grassy banks and

tracks. Long trailing rooting runners. **Flowers** Jun-Sep, single 5-petalled yellow 18-25mm, on long reddish stems; **leaves** long-stalked, palmate with 5-7 toothed leaflets.

TRAILING TORMENTIL
Potentilla anglica
An infrequent sprawling plant with features midway between tormentil and creeping cinquefoil; has 4 or 5 petalled **flowers** with fertile seeds Jun-Sep; **leaves** have 3 or 5 leaflets on stalks which increase in length lower down the plant.

HYBRID CINQUEFOIL
Potentilla x mixta
Sterile hybrids of the above species occasional on verges, woodland rides and waste ground. **Flowers** have 4 or 5 petals; **leaves** with 3 or 5 leaflets but unlike trailing tormentil, leaf-stalks ± equal length throughout the plant.

SILVERWEED *Potentilla anserina*

Common low-growing, stoloniferous perennial with reddish stalks. Mat-forming on tracks, paths, bare and waste ground.

Flowers May-Aug, bright yellow 5-petalled, 15-20mm; **leaves** have pairs of toothed leaflets, green on top and silky white below.

HOARY CINQUEFOIL *Potentilla argentea*

Tangled perennial on free-draining soils, common on the Breckland sands of Norfolk but locally very rare, known only from a grassy lane-side near *Broughton*.

Flowers Jun-Sep, c.10mm; **leaves** with deeply cut lobes, green above, silvery white beneath.

MARSH CINQUEFOIL *Potentilla palustris*

Colourful but uncommon wetland perennial. Upright stems to 50cm grow from creeping rhizomes in non-limy water or marshy ground. **Flowers** Jun-Jul, 20-30mm have 5 or 6 large, pointed, red/purple petals between 5 dark mauve sepals; **leaves** palmate.

PEA FAMILY *FABACEAE*

Flowers have an upright **standard** petal, 2 side **wing** petals and 2 lower petals joined to form a **keel**; tubular calyx with 5 teeth; seeds contained in a pod.

BUSH VETCH *Vicia sepium*

Common perennial on verges and waysides, clambers by tendrils to 1m. **Flowers** May-Nov, pale purple fading to blue 12-15mm, 2-6 on short heads; **leaves** have 5-8 pairs of blunt leaflets; **pod** short, black when ripe.

COMMON VETCH *Vicia sativa*

Downy annual, scrambles widely in grassy and waste places. **Flowers** May-Sep, 10-30mm, single or in pairs, pinkish purple; **leaves** have tendrils and 4-8 pairs narrow leaflets each with end-point; stipules at leaf stalk base have central dark dot; **pod** brown.

TUFTED VETCH *Vicia cracca*

Widespread perennial on rough grassy verges and waysides, scrambling up to 2m. **Flowers** Jun-Aug, 10-12mm, blue/purple, numerous on long slender flowerhead; **leaves** have tendrils and 8-12 pairs of short pointed leaflets; **pod** short, hairless, brown.

SPRING VETCH *Vicia lathyroides*

A tiny sand-dune, low creeping annual, locally rare on the sandy south-eastern fringe of the *Vale of Pickering*. **Flowers** Apr-May, only 5-7mm, solitary, dull purple; **leaves** 2-4 pairs of short leaflets; **fruit** short black pod.

WOOD VETCH *Vicia sylvatica*

Hairless perennial, plentiful on coastal cliffs, scarce inland; scrambles up 2m or more on other vegetation. **Flowers** Jun-Aug, 15-20mm, white, striated purple, up to 15 in lax 1-sided spike; **leaves** 6-10 pairs of leaflets with end-points, fringed stipules, much-branched tendrils; **pod** long, pointed black.

BITHYNIAN VETCH *Vicia bithynica*

Scrambling coastal annual, uncommon throughout UK, has one known site on this coast, *Upgang Ravine,* near *Whitby.* **Flowers** May-Jun, purple and white 16-20mm, two or single on long stalk; **leaves** have prominent toothed stipules, tendrils and 1-2 pairs of broad lancelate leaflets; **pods** brown beaked.

BITTER VETCHLING *Lathyrus linifolius*

Early-flowering perennial of more acidic soils, occasional on heath, lightly-grazed grassland and stream banks. Rather stiff hairy stems erect to 15-40cm. **Flowers** Apr-Jul, 12mm, crimson/red fading blue; **leaves** lack tendrils; 2-4 pairs of pointed narrow leaflets up to 4cm long; **pod** long brown.

MEADOW VETCHLING *Lathyrus pratensis*

Common scrambling perennial, with angled stems 30-120cm; clambers amongst other vegetation on grassy verges, hedgebanks. **Flowers** May-Aug, yellow, 15-18mm in loose heads on long stalks; **leaves** in stalked pairs, long narrow, pointed with parallel veins and tendrils; **pod** black when ripe.

BIRD'S-FOOT
Ornithopus perpusillus
Not to be confused with bird's-foot trefoil, this small rare annual creeps amongst stronger plants in short grassy, sandy ground *Knapton* to *Staxton.* **Flowers** May-Aug, 3-5mm, white, striped pink standard, white wings, yellow keel; leaflets downy; pods beaded and curved, resemble a bird's foot.

HAIRY TARE *Vicia hirsuta*

Drab straggling annual, sometimes abundant on rough or disturbed ground, railtracks. **Flowers** May-Aug, dull mauve, 2-4mm, up to 9 per stem; **leaves** pinnate with 4-10 pairs of narrow leaflets, tendrils branched; **pod** downy, 2-seeded, black when ripe.

SMOOTH TARE *Vicia tetrasperma*
Rare annual near the northern limit of its range, forms untidy small clumps on field edge or rough grassy ground. **Flowers** May-Aug, clear blue/mauve, 4-8mm, 2 or 4 per stem; **leaves** pinnate with 4-6 small leaflets and unbranched tendrils; **pod** 4-seeded hairless, brown when ripe.

KIDNEY VETCH *Anthyllis vulneraria*

Short perennial, common on coastal cliffs, scarce inland; soft hairs give a greyish look. **Flowers** Jun-Sep, small yellow-petalled with white woolly calyx tube, clustered in large globular heads; **leaves** pinnate, up to 6cm, paired narrow, pointed leaflets, green above, downy below.

RESTHARROW *Ononis repens*
Low spreading shrublet grows on coastal boulder clay cliffs and inland on base-rich well-drained soils. **Stems** are <u>hairy all round</u> and with a few soft or no spines. **Flowers** Jun-Sep, 10-15mm, pink/white; **leaves** pinnate, with oval toothed leaflets, very sticky hairy.

SPINY RESTHARROW *Ononis spinosa* is a lowland plant rare in this area; more upright growth, its stems have <u>2 rows of hairs</u> and many sharp spines.

TREE LUPIN *Lupinus arboreus*

Semi-evergreen shrub, long established on a sandy wayside near *Flixton*; short-lived but numerous seedlings maintain a population. **Flowers** May-Aug, yellow, sometimes mauve tinted; many arranged in neat whorls up stems to 2m tall; **leaves** deeply cut palmate, softly hairy beneath.

PURPLE MILK-VETCH *Astragalus danicus*
A low hairy perennial on dunes and thin calcareous grassland; small purple flowers and 6-13 pairs of leaflets; always scarce in this area, it has not been seen on its few known sites for several years.

MELILOTS *Melilotus spp.* grow in scattered groups on less exposed coastal cliffs, uncommon inland. All have long flowering spikes on branched stems to 1.5m tall, trifoliate leaves with long, oval, neatly-toothed leaflets and flower through the summer. **Golden Melilot** *M.altissimus* has golden yellow flowers with equal-sized standard, wing and keel petals; black pods; most frequent.
Ribbed Melilot *M.officinalis* has lemon yellow flowers with keel petals shorter than wings and standard petals; brown pods; **White Melilot** *M.albus* has white flowers; brown pods.

BLACK MEDICK *Medicago lupulina*
Low perennial frequent on dry calcareous grassy banks and
rocky outcrops. **Flowers** Apr-Aug, yellow, tiny, up to 50 in
compact head 3-8mm across; **leaves** trifoliate, leaflets have
small apical point; **pod** tiny black coils in clustered head.

SPOTTED MEDICK *Medicago arabica*
A lowland sprawling annual at its northernmost native site
at *Ruswarp*. **Flowers** Apr-Sep in pairs only 4-6mm; **leaves**
distinctively marked with a dark V, numerous on weak
branched stems which tangle into low bushes; **pod** spiral.

HOP TREFOIL *Trifolium campestre*

Infrequent annual 10-
30cm grows in small
groups on dry
calcareous ground.
Flowers Jun-Sep, pale
yellow with shallow
hood-like standard
petal, many packed into
globular head 10-15mm
across; **leaves** trifoliate;
fruit like tiny hop cone.

LESSER TREFOIL *Trifolium dubium*

Common low
spreading annual in
short turf, lawns and
rocky outcrops;
withstands grazing
and mowing. **Flowers**
Jun-Sep, yellow, tiny,
up to 30 packed into
small head; standard
petals form ridged
covers over pods;
leaves trifoliate,
leaflets straight or
notched at apex.

GORSE *Ulex europaeus*

Evergreen shrub up to 3m, forms dense thickets on coastal cliffs and moorland heaths. **Flowers** yellow 2cm across, fragrant, most appear Apr-Jun, a few any time of the year; **sepals** yellow with spreading hairs; spines furrowed, very sharp; **pod** hairy dark, eject seeds loudly on warm days.

BROOM *Cytisus scoparius*

Spineless shrub with angled wintergreen stems to 2.5m; frequent on dry sandy acidic waysides and heaths. **Flowers** Apr-Jun, deep yellow 2cm; **leaves** 1-3 leaflets, soon fall; **pod** black hairy.

PETTY WHIN *Genista anglica*

Low shrublet scattered in heathy parts of the moor with wiry stems to 1m and short very sharp spines. **Flowers** Apr-Jul, yellow, 7-10mm; **leaves** small oval, pointed; **pod** short, swollen hairless.

DYER'S GREENWEED *Genista tinctoria*

Small deciduous meadow shrub, much reduced by grassland improvement; survives on *Saltwick* cliffs. **Flowers** Jun-Aug, c.15mm in spikes; **leaves** small lanceolate on green twigs; no spines.

BIRD'S-FOOT TREFOIL *Lotus corniculatus*

Attractive widespread perennial, common in meadows and grassy banks except on very acidic ground. Stems to 50cm both creeping and upright. **Flowers** May-Sep, 15mm, bright yellow, reddish in bud, 2-7 in open clusters, <u>calyx teeth erect in bud</u>; **leaves** 3 upper and 2 lower roundish leaflets; **stems** ± solid; **pods** long narrow, brown, splayed like a bird's foot.

GREATER BIRD'S-FOOT TREFOIL *L. pedunculatus* In damp ground and grassy streamsides, this plant replaces common bird's-foot trefoil. Stem is more upright to 1m, hairy, usually hollow; **Flowers** later, Jul-Aug, deeper yellow; <u>calyx teeth spreading</u> in bud; **leaves** hairy.

KNOTTED CLOVER *Trifolium striatum*

Rare in NE Yorks. A low winter annual, sprawls on disturbed sandy ground around *Ganton*. **Flowerheads** Jun-Jul, small ovoid, stalkless, partly enclosed by stipules with prominent red veins; **leaves** trifoliate, downy on both sides.

HARE'S-FOOT CLOVER *Trifolium arvense*

Locally rare annual on sandy heath or rail ballast; spreads to form dense patches. **Flowerheads** Jun-Sep, dusky pink, softly hairy, stalked, on branched stems to 30cm; tiny white florets; **leaflets** narrow.

RED CLOVER *Trifolium pratense*

Common native perennial in grassland. **Flowers** May-Nov, deep pink with white base, packed in globular heads <u>close to stem leaves</u> below; **leaves** trifoliate with red striated stipules; pale curved mark on oval leaflets. *Ssp sativa* which is planted in short-term grass leys has brighter flowers and few leaf markings.

ZIG-ZAG CLOVER *Trifolium medium*

Occasional perennial on grassy verges, banks and streamsides with heavy soils; slightly zig-zag stems erect to 40cm. **Flowers** Jun-Sep, dark pink/red, clustered in roundish head c.30mm; <u>stem leaves usually distant</u> from flowerhead; **leaves** trifoliate with pointed stipules; faint or no pale mark on narrow leaflet.

WHITE CLOVER *Trifolium repens*

Creeping perennial widespread in shorter grassy ground where it tolerates mowing and grazing. Various cultivars are sown in managed grassland. **Flowers** Jun-Sep, white, small, packed in roundish heads c.20mm on long stalks; brownish withered heads persist; **leaves** trifoliate, leaflets almost round, marked with faint white V.

ALSIKE CLOVER *Trifolium hybridum*

Annual sometimes sown in grass mixtures, naturalises occasionally on rough open ground. **Flowers** Jun-Sep, white/pink in short-stalked heads; **leaves** trifoliate unmarked.

WILLOWHERB FAMILY *ONAGRACEAE*

Perennials with 4-petalled pink flowers; type of stigma assists species identification. Hybridisation is frequent.

Stigmas 4-lobed:

ROSEBAY   *Chamerion angustifolium*

Rare upland plant two centuries ago, rosebay is now common in most of the UK, forming extensive stands on verges, clearings and wasteland. **Flowers** Jun-Sep, 20-30mm across; numerous on leafy spikes up to 1.5m tall; unequal-sized petals and long spreading sepals, both pink; **stigma** 4-lobed; **leaves** narrow lanceolate.

BROAD-LEAVED WILLOWHERB
Epilobium montanum

Flowers Jun-Aug, 12-15mm; pink notched petals and drooping buds; **stigma** 4-lobed; stem round, erect to 75cm; **leaves** broad, toothed, rounded at the base, short-stalked. Common on bare ground.

GREAT WILLOWHERB   *Epilobium hirsutum*

Frequent, greyish and often widespread perennial in damp places and along streamsides; has brightly-

coloured flowers and dense soft foliage. **Flowers** Jul-Aug, 15-23mm across, petals purple-pink, notched, equal-sized; **stigma** 4 recurved lobes; stems up to 2m tall, branched; **leaves** stalkless, very hairy, part clasp the stem.

HOARY WILLOWHERB   *Epilobium parviflorum*

Frequent greyish hairy plant in damp soils on streamsides, old quarries, waste. **Flowers** Jul-Sep, pink 7-12mm, petals deeply notched; **stigma** 4 non-curved lobes; stem to 80cm; **leaves** covered with white hairs.

Stigmas club:

AMERICAN WILLOWHERB
Epilobium ciliatum
A rarity before 1940, now common on disturbed ground, footpaths, in gardens; often hybridises with other willowherbs. **Flowers** Jun-Aug, 4-6mm, pale pink notched petals widely spaced; **stigma** club-shaped; stems to 1m reddish, have 4 raised lines near the top and many crisped, appressed and glandular hairs; **leaves** lanceolate, short-stalked.

MARSH WILLOWHERB
Epilobium palustre
Frequent in marshes and wet moorlands, avoiding calcareous ground. **Flowers** Jul-Aug, small, pale pink or white, 4-6mm often drooping; **stigma** club-shaped; stems round, often with crisped hairs; erect to 60cm from a curved base; **leaves** strap-shaped, almost stalkless.

SHORT-FRUITED WILLOWHERB
Epilobium obscurum
Frequent in damp or disturbed ground. **Flowers** Jul-Aug, 7-9mm pink, buds erect; **stigma** club-shaped; glandular hairs on sepals; stem to 80cm tall from a curving base has 4 raised lines, appressed hairs; forms long stolons; **leaves** blunt tipped, rounded stalkless base; pod short on longish stalk.

PALE WILLOWHERB
Epilobium roseum
Lowland plant, infrequent in damp woodland edge, disturbed ground.
Flowers Jul-Aug, 4-6mm pale pink; buds white; **stigma** club-shaped; stem 25-80cm has 2 strong and 2 obscure raised lines, glandular hairs at top; **leaves** stalked.

SQUARE-STALKED WILLOWHERB
Epilobium tetragonum
Occasional stiff, upright plant in damp soils, streamsides. Square stems 30-70cm, mostly hairless below but with appressed hairs above; no glandular hairs. **Flowers** Jul-Aug, 6-8mm; **stigma** club-shaped; **leaves** unstalked, strap-shaped, coarsely toothed, look greasy or shiny, run into wings on the stem.

NEW ZEALAND WILLOWHERB
Epilobium brunnescens

New Zealand native, first recorded in the wild in UK in 1904, now scattered in the uplands. Forms tangled mats on damp open ground, ditches, gravelly tracks, moist walls. **Flowers** May-Oct, 3-4mm, pale pink or white, single on long erect stalk; stems prostrate, creeping and rooting; **leaves** small, almost round, short-stalked.

ENCHANTER'S NIGHTSHADE
Circaea lutetiana

Frequent patch-forming perennial in shady woodland, hedgebanks and scrub on nutrient-rich soils. **Flowers** Jun-Aug, 2 tiny petals, deeply cleft; stems erect to 50cm; **leaves** dull above, shiny below, large, pointed; **fruit** small oval covered with white hooked bristles.

DOGWOOD FAMILY *CORNACEAE*

DWARF CORNEL *Cornus suecica*

An arctic plant widespread in the Scottish Highlands, has its most southerly UK site near *Saltergate* in NE Yorks. A 12,000 year-old legacy from the last ice age, it is scattered beneath bracken and bilberry on north-facing slopes. **Flowers** Jun-Sep; 4 large white bracts surround a cluster of tiny dark purple flowers on rarely branched stems up to 25cm tall; **leaves** in opposite pairs have prominent convergent parallel veins; **fruit** a red berry.

DOGWOOD *Cornus sanguinea*

Deciduous large lowland shrub on lime-rich soils, occasional in hedgerows and scrub woodland away from the moors. **Flowers** Jun-Jul, small, creamy white, 4-petalled, in terminal clusters; **leaves** oval, pointed, with prominent converging parallel veins, in opposite stalked pairs; stems branched, turn red in the autumn as do the leaves; **fruit** a black berry.

SPINDLE FAMILY CELASTRACEAE

SPINDLE *Euonymous europaeus*

Deciduous open small tree, infrequent in sparse woodland on limestone. **Flowers** May-Jun, small 4-petalled greenish in sprays; **leaves** oval, stalked pairs on green 4-angled twigs; **fruit** 4 bright pink lobes surround seeds with shiny, orange, fleshy coverings.

OLIVE FAMILY OLEAECAE

WILD PRIVET *Ligustrum vulgare*

Semi-evergreen shrub, occasional in hedgerows, scrub on non-acid soils; bushes up to 3m tall. **Flowers** Jun-Jul, funnel-shaped, massed in short spikes; black shiny berries; **leaves** narrow oval. (garden privet, a widely planted Japanese shrub, has broad oval leaves).

MEZEREON FAMILY THYMELAEACEAE

SPURGE LAUREL *Daphne laureola*

Evergreen lowland shrub 1-2m tall, uncommon in old deciduous shady woods on non-acid soils. **Flowers** Feb-Apr, yellow-green, 4-petalled funnel, slightly fragrant; **leaves** large, oval, shiny green, leathery; shiny black berry.

MEZEREON *Daphne mezereum*

Deciduous early native and garden shrub. Origin of plants in an old limestone quarry at *Saintoft* is unknown. **Flowers** Jan-Apr, 4-petalled tubular, very fragrant, appear before leaves; **leaves** light green lanceolate; shiny red berry.

BARBERRY FAMILY *BERBERIDACEAE*

BARBERRY *Berberis vulgaris*
Formerly frequent in hedges but its ability to host a cereal rust led to its removal from most arable areas; now rare in coppice or scrub; small deciduous tree to 4m; twigs with 3-pronged spines.
Flowers
Jun-July, yellow
5-petalled bells
6-8mm hang in
sprays; **leaves**
small oval,
prickle-edged;
fruit oval red
berries 8-12mm.

SEA-BUCKTHORN FAMILY *ELEAGNACEA*

SEA-BUCKTHORN
Hippophea rhamnoides
Spiny coastal shrub, scarce except where planted in amenity schemes. Extensive suckers and dense-branching form thorny, impenetrable thickets. Tiny **flowers** have 2 sepals but no petals, Apr-Jun before the leaves; bright orange berries in autumn; **leaves** narrow strap-like, grey/green above, brownish beneath.

SPURGE FAMILY *EUPHORBIACEAE*

Herbs with alternate simple leaves; stems contain milky latex in spurge, watery latex in mercury.

DOG'S MERCURY *Mercurialis perennis*
Dioecious hairy perennial, 15-40cm forms dense, short, dark green ground-cover in old damp woodland; spreads extensively by rhizomes. **Flowers** Feb-May, petal-less in small groups on erect green spikes; male have numerous yellow stamens above triangular sepals; female stalked on separate plants;
rounded ovary
forms 2-celled
hairy fruit; **leaves**
oval pointed,
finely toothed.

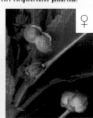

ANNUAL MERCURY
Mercurialis annua
Southern dioecious annual, locally rare in nutrient-rich, disturbed soils. Differs from dog's mercury by flowering later, Apr-Aug, and almost hairless paler foliage; female flowers almost stalkless. Produces long-lived seeds – some were found in York's Viking site excavation.
Whitby

Spurges have milky stem juice (latex) and prominent glands on yellow/green flowers; simple oval leaves.

PETTY SPURGE *Euphorbia peplus*

Hairless annual, erect and branched to 20cm, common on waste, pathside and cultivated ground. **Flowerheads** Apr-Nov, 3-rayed, pea-green; flowers consist of small cups, each with long-horned semi-circular glands, tiny stamens and a stalked round ovary and stigma.

SUN SPURGE *Euphorbia helioscopa*

Yellowish, hairless annual c. 30cm, common on disturbed, sunny ground. **Flowerheads** May-Oct, rather flat, 5 rayed; flowers are small cups topped by kidney-shaped glands without horns, tiny stamens and a stalked round ovary and stigma; **leaves** blunt oval, slightly toothed.

DWARF SPURGE
Euphorbia exigua
Small spindly annual 5-15cm, rare on arable land with dry, nutrient-rich soils. **Flowers** Jun-Oct, consist of small cup topped with kidney-shaped glands with long slender horns; **leaves** small, narrow, pointed.

MOSCHATEL FAMILY *ADOXACEAE*

MOSCHATEL or TOWNHALL CLOCK
Adoxa moschatellina
Early short, unobtrusive but widespread perennial, creeps far on shady verges, wood edge. **Flowers** Mar-May, yellow/green, tiny, 4 face outwards, one upwards, on slender stalks to 15cm; **leaves** thin, 3 lobed, leaflets with blunt, shallow lobes.

BOGBEAN FAMILY *MENYANTHACEAE*

BOGBEAN *Menyanthes trifoliata*

Far-spreading aquatic perennial occasional in pools, bogs and slow-moving water. **Flowers** May-Jul, have 5 fringed petals opening from a long tube, pink in bud, white when open; fleshy stems up to 30cm above the water; **leaves** tough, long-stalked, with 3 large blunt oval leaflets.

WOOD SORREL FAMILY *OXALIDACEAE*

WOOD SORREL *Oxalis acetosella*

Elegant small creeping perennial, frequent in damp woodland and on shady hedgebanks. **Flowers** Apr-May, 10-20 mm, 5 white or pink petals, striated violet, yellow centre; **leaves** clover-like, green above, often purple beneath.

FLAX FAMILY *LINACEAE*

FAIRY FLAX *Linum catharticum* Slender low annual, plentiful on bare forest rides, heath and short grassland. **Flowers** Jun-Sept, 4-6mm, 5 white petals, yellow stamens, solitary on thin short stems; **leaves** small oval, 1-veined, in pairs.

IVY FAMILY ARALIACEAE

COMMON IVY *Hedera helix*

Evergreen woody climber or ground carpeter, very common on trees, walls and in dry woods. Stems with clinging roots can reach 30m; **leaves** on non-flowering stems palmate, 3-5 lobed with pale hairs beneath; older stems have more ovoid leaves and in good light produce bunches of 5-petalled greenish **flowers** Sep-Nov; dull black winter berries.

BALSAM FAMILY BALSAMINACEAE

HIMALAYAN BALSAM *Impatiens glandulifera*

Introduced for gardens in C19 from the Himalayas, now a troublesome waterside invader. Stem 1-2m tall, succulent, ridged. **Flowers** Jul-Oct, 2-4cm long, short curved spur; **leaves** large, toothed; **fruit** pear-shaped, explodes to disperse seeds afar.

ORANGE BALSAM *Impatiens capensis*

Annual, introduced in C19, naturalised on canals, ponds and riverbanks. Locally rare. Hairless stems to 1m or more, swollen nodes. **Flowers** Jul-Aug, 2-3mm orange, red-spotted, with curved spur; **leaves** stalked, oval, toothed; capsules eject seeds.

CRANE'S-BILL FAMILY GERANIACEAE

Flowers pink, mauve or blue with 5 petals, usually striated; wide range of flower size; fruits shaped liked a bird's long narrow beak, 5 segments curl upwards to release ripe seeds.

MEADOW CRANE'S-BILL *Geranium pratense*

Large bushy perennial up to 1m with branched hairy stems; frequent on verges, railside and rough grassland with non-acidic soil. **Flowers** Jun-Sep, blue 30-40mm in pairs; **leaves** palmate, lobes deeply toothed; fruits hairy, wrinkled, hang down.

BLOODY CRANE'S-BILL *Geranium sanguineum*

Rare bushy perennial, grows on a coastal cliff and inland on a few limestone outcrops. **Flowers** Jul-Aug, up to 40mm across, a striking deep pink/mauve with dark stamens; single-flowered stems; **leaves** deeply cut into many linear segments. *Filey, Murton, Arden.*

DUSKY CRANE'S-BILL *Geranium phaeum*

Introduced as a garden perennial and naturalised in a few rather shady locations. **Flowers** May-Sep, up to 30mm across, dark purple, white-centred, on hairy stems erect to 70cm; **leaves** on stems and from the ground have up to 5 palmate, toothed lobes. *Hawnby, Old Byland,*

HEDGEROW CRANE'S-BILL *Geranium pyrenaicum*

Downy much branched perennial 25-60cm; infrequent in straggly spreads on road verges and in rough grassland. **Flowers** Jun-Aug, strong purple, 15-20mm, in pairs, petals notched; **leaves** long-stalked, hairy, ± circular, deeply lobed with shallow indented edge; fruit downy, smooth.

CUT-LEAVED CRANE'S-BILL *Geranium dissectum*

Short spreading annual differs from dove's-foot crane's-bill by its hairy fruit and leaf shape. Frequent in arable fields, gardens, meadows. **Flowers** May-Aug, pink 8-10mm; petals notched, show bristle-pointed sepals between; **leaves** deeply divided into narrow linear lobes, hairy; fruit hairy.

DOVE'S-FOOT CRANE'S-BILL *Geranium molle*

Common in cultivated ground, dry grassland. A short, often prostrate annual, densely covered with fine white hairs. **Flowers** Apr-Sep, pink 6-10mm, anthers purple, petals notched; sepals blunt; **leaves** ± circular, indented, softly hairy; fruit hairless, wrinkled.

SMALL-FLOWERED CRANE'S-BILL *Geranium pusillum*

Short, often ground-hugging downy annual, infrequent on dry grassland, sandy waste. **Flowers** Jun-Sep, pale mauve 4-6mm, with 5 fertile and 5 sterile stamens, petals notched; **leaves** roundish, cut into 5 bluntly-toothed lobes; fruit downy, smooth.

SHINING CRANE'S-BILL *Geranium lucidum*

Unusual annual on limestone outcrops and walls. Hairless, fleshy stems 10-40cm, break easily. **Flowers** May-Aug, deep pink 10-14mm, petals not notched; **leaves** long-stalked, shiny, green or red, ± circular, deeply lobed, shallow blunt teeth.

HERB-ROBERT *Geranium robertianum*

Common in various habitats and soils - old quarries, gardens and waysides, usually in light shade. A reddish, hairy annual 10-40cm tall, often overwintering. **Flowers** Apr-Sep, 14-18mm, deep pink with orange or purple anthers, petals spaced, blunt not notched; **leaves** triangular in outline, lobes deeply blunt-toothed; smell when bruised.

COMMON STORK'S-BILL *Erodium cicutarium*

Prostrate or sprawling annual, occasional on dry sandy or stony soils, rail ballast. **Flowers** Apr-Sep, rose-pink 6-18mm, 10 stamens (only 5 fertile); petals unequal, two smaller have black spot at base; **leaves** pinnate with leaflets deeply toothed; fruits have beaks up to 4cm long

which twist spirally to release ripe seeds.

PENCILLED CRANE'S-BILL *Geranium versicolour*

is a garden escape which establishes infrequently on verges or wasteland, usually near habitation. **Flowers** 24-28mm May-Aug; **leaves** deeply divided.

LONG-STALKED CRANE'S-BILL

Geranium columbinum
Erect plant, rare on lime-rich grassy ground; reddish stem to 60 cm has solitary **flower**, May-Aug, 12-18mm; bristle-ended sepals; **leaves** deeply divided.

MILKWORT FAMILY *POLYGALACEAE*

Prostrate or low perennial in short grassland; creeping or upright stems to 30cm. **Flowers** May-Sep, shaped like small inflated tubes, consist of 3 tiny green sepals at the base of 2 large coloured sepals; inside these lies a fringed, projecting small tube of 3 pale petals; **leaves** small, oval.

COMMON MILKWORT

Polygala vulgaris
Flowers vary blue, mauve, white or pink, 4-7mm; **all leaves alternate** on stems. Common on dry acid or lime-rich unimproved grassland.

HEATH MILKWORT

Polygala serpyllifolia
Flowers deep blue or pink, 5-6mm; **lower leaves opposite.** Occasional on acid heath, avoids lime.

CARROT FAMILY APIACEAE

Large family, known
collectively as umbellifers.
Small, mainly white flowers,
stalked to form a flat or
domed umbrella type head.
Includes several tall showy
roadside plants.
Shape of fruit, presence of
bracts and bracteoles on the
umbel and flowering time
important for identification.

COW PARSLEY Anthriscus sylvestris

Also known as Queen
Annne's lace, common
on verges, field edge
and in grassy places.
Erect branched
perennial to 1m or more.
Stem hollow, unspotted,
downy below; umbels to
6cm diam. with
bracteoles but
no bracts Apr-
Jun; **fruit** 6mm
long, smooth,
oblong.

ROUGH CHERVIL Chaerophyllum temulem

Tall, branched biennial,
common on road verges,
flowering after cow
parsley. Stem solid,
ridged, hairy, purple-
spotted, swollen at
nodes; umbels 3-6cm,
rather irregular,
bracts 0-2,
bracteoles 5-8,
Jun-Jul; **fruit**
c.6mm long,
smooth, oblong.

BUR CHERVIL Anthriscus caucalis

Rare annual on sandy or
gravelly soils in
grassland or arable
fields. Stem to 70m,
hairless, hollow; **flowers**
small white, 3-6mm on
spreading stalks, May-
Jun; **leaves** finely cut,
pale green, appear
feathery; **fruit**
c 3mm oval,
covered with
short hooked
bristles.

UPRIGHT HEDGE PARSLEY *Torilis japonica*

Branched, late-flowering annual to 1m tall, frequent on verges and rough non-acidic grassland. **Stem** solid, unspotted, rough with appressed straight hairs. **Flowers** white or pink, in umbels to 4cm across, have bracts and bracteoles, Jul-Sep; **fruits** 4mm covered with <u>hooked hairs</u>.

KNOTTED HEDGE-PARSLEY *Torilis nodosa*

A southern slender annual, erect or sprawling to 30cm; locally rare on arable and dry open ground. **Flowers** tiny 2-3mm in tight umbels May-Jul.

Leaves finely cut, pale green, softly hairy; dense cluster of warty <u>straight-spined</u> fruits.

SWEET CICELY *Myrrhis odorata*

Mainly northern perennial, smells of aniseed, spreads on verges, river banks. **Stem** hollow, downy, grooved; **flowers** creamy white, umbels to 8cm, no bracts, 5 bracteoles Jun-Jul; **leaves** often blotched; **fruit** 20-25mm long, sharply ridged, dark, shiny brown when ripe.

HEMLOCK *Conium maculatum*

Poisonous tall biennial, frequent in rough grassland, on verges, disturbed and waste ground; large plant with musty smell and feathery foliage. **Stems hollow,** to 2m tall, hairless, purple-spotted; umbels 2-6cm, bracts reflexed, few bracteoles, Jun-Jul; **leaves** finely dissected, often yellowish-green; **fruit** globular 3mm has wavy ridges.

ANGELICA *Angelica sylvestris*

Stout, hairless, moisture-loving perennial up to 2m tall. Widespread on rough damp ground. **Stem** hollow, purplish, ridged, large sheathing bracts at nodes; **flowers** Jun-Sep, white/pink, domed umbel 3-15cm, no bracts, few bracteoles; large **leaves** have toothed leaflets; **fruit** flat oval 5mm long, winged.

HOGWEED *Heracleum sphondylium*

Robust, hairy biennial to 2m tall, plentiful on coarse grassy verges, coastal cliffs. **Stem** hollow, ridged hairy; **flowers** Jun-Sep white or pink, petals notched unequal, umbels 5-15cm, bracteoles but no bracts; **leaves** coarse grey-green, unevenly lobed, leaf base clasps stem; **fruit** long oval, flat, smooth, dark lined.

ALEXANDERS *Smyrnium olusatrum*

Large biennial, plentiful along the coast, rare inland. Smells of celery. **Stems** tough, furrowed, hollow with age; **flowers** Mar-Jun, only 1-5mm yellow, in large domed umbels; **leaves** yellow/green, cut into large, toothed, hairy leaflets; **fruit** black 6-8mm.

GIANT HOGWEED *Heracleum mantegazzianum*

An oversize version of hogweed which can reach 5m tall. Introduced from Asia as a garden feature in the early C19th, it soon took to the wild. Known to cause severe skin irritation, it is being eradicated wherever possible.

GREATER BURNET-SAXIFRAGE *Pimpinella major*
Mainly in the western part of the area, frequent on road verges and wood edges. Robust hairless perennial grows in large leafy clumps. **Stem** to 120cm, hollow, ridged; **flowers** Jun-Jul, white in almost flat umbels 3-6 cm, no bracts or bracteoles; **leaves** large, dark green, glossy.

BURNET-SAXIFRAGE *Pimpinella saxifraga*
Slender, upright, branched perennial frequent in grassy habitats on well-drained, more calcareous soils. **Stem** tough, ridged, solid, to 70cm; **flowers** May-Sep, white in umbels 2-5 cm, no bracts or bracteoles; **leaves** basal long-stalked with paired small oval toothed leaflets, stem leaves have short linear leaflets; **fruit** shiny.

FOOL'S PARSLEY *Aethusa cynapium*
Low hairless annual to 50cm occasional on arable and waste land. **Flowers** Jun-Oct, white in umbels 2-6cm; conspicuous narrow bracteoles 1cm long hang down, no bracts; **leaves** dark green, fern-like; **fruit** oval with broad ridges.

PIGNUT *Conopodium majus*
Short perennial, frequent in pastures, copses, verges. Slender upright flower stems to 40cm from underground small edible tubers. **Flowers** May-Jun, white, in umbels 3-7cm; bracts and bracteoles few or none; **leaves** triangular in outline, finely divided into numerous narrow segments; **fruit** 4mm oval, retains erect style.

WILD CARROT *Daucus carota*

Hairy biennial on more calcareous soils, mainly coastal. Solid, ridged stems to 1m tall. **Flowers** Jun-Aug, pinkish white (central flower often dark red); umbel 3-7cm across, saucer-shaped when mature; bracts long narrow, lobed, form fringe beneath flowers; **leaves** divided into toothed leaflets; **fruit** 4mm oval, ridged spiny.

WOOD SANICLE *Sanicula europaea*

Frequent, patch-forming, hairless perennial 20-60cm tall in lime-rich woodland. **Flowers** May-Aug, dull white, tiny, packed into small ball-type umbels; bracteoles obscure, bracts divided; **leaves** long-stalked from the ground with almost circular blades deeply lobed, toothed, shiny; smaller stem leaves; **fruit** round with hooked spines.

PEPPER-SAXIFRAGE *Silaum silaus*

Rare shrubby perennial in damp grassland. **Stems** to 1m, slender, ridged, branched. **Flowers** Jun-Aug, dull yellow in widely-spaced umbels 2-6cm; bracteoles linear, no bracts; **leaves** finely divided into long narrow leaflets; **fruits** oval, smooth, shiny.

Upgang, Cropton, Raindale, Gerrick

WILD CELERY *Apium graveolens*

Coastal biennial, rare on cliffs at *Staithes* and saltmarsh at *Ruswarp*. Smells of celery when crushed. Solid branched stems to 1m. **Flowers** Jun-Aug, white, in uneven umbels, no bracts or bracteoles; **leaves** yellow/green, shiny, with large, flat, toothed leaflets.

SHEPHERD'S-NEEDLE *Scandix pecten-veneris*

Short cornfield annual, named after its very long slender beaked fruits. Rare on arable land. **Flowers** May-July, white, tiny in tight 1cm umbels with pointed bracteoles; **leaves** finely divided; **fruits** up to 7cm long have stiff needle-like beaks.

GROUND-ELDER *Aegopodium podagraria*

Extensive perennial, common on verges, waste ground, gardens. **Stem** to 1m tall stout, hollow, grooved. **Flowers** May-Jul, only 1mm; umbels 2-6cm across, no bracts or bracteoles; **leaves** pale, lobed to form a 'thumb'; **fruit** ovoid, ridged.

HEMLOCK WATER DROPWORT *Oenanthe crocata*

Poisonous perennial infrequent on coastal cliiffs and marsh around *Whitby* and *Cayton*, rare inland. Forms robust leafy clumps to 1.5m with hollow ridged stems; **flowers** Jun-Jul, 2mm in long-stalked umbels 5-10cm across; red stamens; linear bracts and bracteoles; **fruit** oval, retains long styles.

FOOL'S WATERCRESS *Apium nodiflorum*

Sprawling yellow/green aquatic, frequent by stream, ditch or pond edge. **Flowers** Jun-Sep, white, in umbels 2-3cm on upright stems; few or no bracts but 5 bracteoles beneath the sepals; **leaves** bright green, shiny, in 3-6 neatly toothed pairs.

LESSER WATER-PARSNIP *Berula erecta*

Poisonous aquatic perennial, occasional on stream-side and in marshes on lower ground; erect and spreading to 1m with hollow stems. **Flowers** Jul-Sep, white in open umbels 3-6cm, prominent leaf-like bracts and bracteoles; **leaves** bluish green, 7-14 pairs of coarsely toothed leaflets.

ring mark usually shows part way up leaf stalk.

LESSER MARSHWORT
Apium inundatum
Uncommon small perennial in shallow ponds or marsh. **Flowers** Jun-Aug, white in few small umbels 1-3cm across; pinnate surface **leaves** with deeply toothed leaflets, submerged leaves with narrow linear leaflets.

MARSH PENNYWORT
Hydrocotyle vulgaris
Creeping or floating wetland perennial, extensive in marsh and fens. **Flowers** Jun-Aug, greenish, only 1mm, in tiny clusters on short stalks, hard to find secreted amongst leaves; **leaves** shallow-toothed almost circular blades, grow flat on centre stalk.

FLOATING PENNYWORT
Hydrocotyle ranunculoides
Troublesome recent introduction spreads rapidly to clog up waterways. An attempt is being made to eradicate it from *Scarborough* and *Throxenby Meres*. Differs from marsh pennywort by crenate leaf blades and stalk at the blade side, not central.

GENTIAN FAMILY *GENTIANACEAE*

Short colourful plants with opposite unstalked leaves; flower tube opens in bright weather with 4-8 petals.

COMMON CENTAURY *Centaurium erythraea*

Elegant biennial, occasionally in large numbers in old quarries, on well-drained forest rides and bare ground. Stems 8-30cm, branched, hairless; **flowers** Jun-Oct, 5-petalled star-like, shell-pink 10-12mm, few in flat stem-top clusters; **leaves** oval, in ground rosette and neat pairs up stems.

YELLOW-WORT *Blackstonia perfoliata*

A distinctive short annual or biennial on moist basic soils. Frequent on sea cliffs but rare inland. **Flowers** Jun-Oct, 10-15mm across have 6-8 equal petals; small clusters on stems upright to 50cm; **leaves** greyish, pointed oval, parallel veined, in ground rosette and clasping the stem in pairs.

AUTUMN GENTIAN or FELWORT *Gentianella amarella*

Erect annual or biennial 3 to 30cm tall. Occasionally numerous on basic soils, in limestone grassland, heath and old quarries. **Flowers** Aug-Sep, 10mm across with 4 or 5 pointed, dusky-purple or pink petals joined to form a tube; calyx tube has ± equal narrow pointed sepals; **leaves** lanceolate, often purplish.

Field Gentian *Gentianella campestris* is a similar plant of more acid soils. Always scarce, has not been found locally since 1970s. It has 4 petals and calyx with 2 wide and 2 narrow sepal lobes. **Marsh Gentian** *Gentiana pneumonanthe* grew in marshes near *Keldy* until 1980s when the land was drained. No other local site is known.

BINDWEED FAMILY *CONVOLVULACEAE*

LARGE BINDWEED *Calystegia silvatica*
Glabrous perennial, introduced in the C19, now
widespread. Long climbing stems festoon hedges.
Flowers Jun-Oct, large
trumpet 6-7cm across
with long tube; <u>sepals
almost hidden by 2 large
inflated bracts</u>; **leaves**
large, triangular with
rounded lower lobes.

HEDGE BINDWEED
Calystegia sepium
Like large bindweed but
has smaller trumpet 3-
4cm across; <u>sepals show between bracts which are
scarcely inflated</u>. Although this is a native species, it is
not common locally, growing mainly near the coast.

HAIRY BINDWEED
Calystegia pulchra
Garden climber naturalised
rarely on hedgerows.
Flowers Jun-Oct, 4-6cm,
bright pink, with 5 <u>narrow</u>
white stripes. Leaf and
flower stalks softly hairy;
bracts inflated and
overlapping, ± hiding the
calyx.

FIELD BINDWEED
Convolvulus arvensis
Persistent low scrambler on
fences, rocks, verges;
extensive ground cover
frequent on waste and railsides. **Flowers** Jun-Sept;
trumpets 3cm across, pink
with 5 <u>wide</u> white stripes;
leaves pointed oval with
arrow-shaped base.

DODDER FAMILY *CUSCUTACEAE*

DODDER *Cuscuta epithymum*   Parasitic climber without green chlorophyll, usually
annual. Long twining
thread-like red
stems tangle over
host vegetation –
gorse, clovers,
rockrose etc.
Flowers Jul-Sep,
tiny 5-lobed bells 3-
4mm packed into
small roundish
heads c.10mm;
leaves merely tiny
scales.
Southern plant
locally very rare,
occurs in *Gundale*,
north of Pickering.

NIGHTSHADE FAMILY *SOLANACEAE*

Plants with 5 similar petals, often brightly coloured. Usually poisonous in parts.

DUKE OF ARGYLL'S TEAPLANT
Lycium barbarum

BITTERSWEET or WOODY NIGHTSHADE
Solanum dulcamara

Introduced by mistake for tea plant, naturalised infrequently in hedges, on walls and waste. Stems to 3m long, spiny, arching to form tangled mass. **Flowers** Jun-Sep, 5-petalled with column of yellow anthers 10-15mm; **leaves** long pointed oval leathery; berry red.

Clambering perennial forms spreading open small bushes, often near water. Scattered but nowhere frequent. **Flowers** Jun-Sep, 10-15mm, 5 bright purple, pointed, reflexed petals surround a column of yellow stamens; **leaves** long broad oval with 2 spreading lobes at base; berries shiny, red, oval, hang in bunches.

BLACK NIGHTSHADE *Solanum nigrum*
Uncommon annual at the northern end of its range, grows on disturbed or waste ground, sprawling or erect to 70cm. **Flowers** Jul-Sep, c.12mm, white 5-petalled with column of yellow stamens; **leaves** hairy or glabrous; berry black.

DEADLY NIGHTSHADE *Atropa belladonna*
Formerly cultivated as a medicinal herb, but fatal if ill-used. A southern plant locally very rare. Grows up to 2m tall in scrub or disturbed ground on lime. **Flowers** Jun-Aug, solitary, up to 3cm across; **leaves** large pointed oval; fruit a large shiny black berry.

HENBANE *Hyocyamus niger*

Foetid biennial to 80cm tall, rare on light soils, highly poisonous. **Flowers** Jun-Aug, 2-3cm diam, often purple veined; **leaves** glandular hairy, roughly toothed; fruit a capsule 1-2cm opens at the top.

THORN APPLE *Datura stramonium*
Sturdy annual, formerly cultivated to treat asthma, now a rare casual to 1m tall on disturbed ground.

Flowers Jul-Oct, white or purple, 4-5 cm, solitary, **leaves** large with pointed lobes; fruit ovoid prickly capsule 4-5cm gives the plant its name.

BORAGE FAMILY *BORAGINACEAE*

Hairy plants with 5-petalled flowers, wheel or bell-shaped, 5-toothed calyx; buds usually in a coiled spike.

VIPER'S BUGLOSS *Echium vulgare*

Uncommon biennial on well-drained soils in grassy or disturbed ground and old quarries. Erect stems to 80cm, covered with reddish bristles. **Flowers** Jun-Sep, trumpet-shaped, 5 unequal bright blue petals, protruding pink stamens; **leaves** strap-shaped, prominent mid vein.

GREEN ALKANET *Pentaglottis sempervirens*

Garden introduction, frequently naturalised on verges and near habitation. Robust, hairy, bushy perennial; branched rough stems to 1m. **Flowers** Mar-Jul, wheel-shaped, 10mm across, strong blue, white-centred; 5 equal petals; **leaves** rough, deep veining, large oval, pale beneath.

COMMON GROMWELL *Lithospermum officinale*

Locally rare perennial reaching its northern limit. Grows in small groups of rough, hairy branched stems to 1m tall in wood edge and scrub grassland on base-rich soil. **Flowers** Jun-Jul, wheel-shaped 3-6mm across, greenish-yellow, 5-petalled; **leaves** long lanceolate, stalkless up the stem with

several conspicuous veins; fruit oval 3mm hard, almost silvery white.

Newtondale

CORN GROMWELL
Lithospermum arvense
has white flowers and a single prominent leaf vein; seeds brown. Rare short-lived annual on arable fields, occasionally introduced with seed-corn.

ABRAHAM, ISAAC and JACOB
Trachystemon orientalis

A Caucasian perennial brought to British gardens in the C18th, naturalised infrequently. **Flowers** Mar-May, 15mm, 5 petals curl back to expose column of stamens; large crinkly oval **leaves** enlarge as flowers die back. Grows on a verge near *Rievaulx* and a streamside at *Stainsacre*.

BUGLOSS *Anchusa arvensis*

Introduced annual appears occasionally on field margins of light arable land. Erect bristly branched plant up to 50cm. **Flowers** Jun-Sep, bright blue 5-petalled c.5mm; **leaves** oblong with wavy margins, covered with bristly hairs.

FIDDLENECK *Amsinckia micrantha*

Introduced American annual resembling a rough, hairy, yellow-flowered forget-me-not, appears erratically but often in large swathes on arable land with light sandy soil. **Flowers** Apr-Aug, open as the stem uncoils; small 5-petalled with hairy calyx; **leaves** rough bristly.

BORAGE *Borago officinalis*

From garden plants and bird seed, this colourful annual infrequently establishes briefly in the wild. Also sown occasionally as a commercial crop. **Flowers** May-Sep, 8-16mm bright blue, reflexed petals surround column of stamens; **leaves** rough, oval, wavy-edged.

WOOD FORGET-ME-NOT
Myosotis sylvatica

forget-me-nots on dry land

FIELD FORGET-ME-NOT
Myosotis arvensis

Frequent native perennial on damp, fertile soils in woods, shady grassland, quarries, augmented by garden throw-outs. Spreading branched hairy stems to 50cm; **flowers** Apr-Aug, <u>6-10mm across, flat</u>; petals <u>longer</u> than their tube; **leaves** oval, downy.

Common annual or biennial on open grassy or bare or cultivated ground; spreading branched hairy stems to 40cm; **flowers** Apr-Sep, to <u>5mm across, saucer-shaped</u>; petals <u>shorter</u> than their tube; **leaves** oval, downy.

EARLY FORGET-ME-NOT *Myosotis ramosissima*

Small annual, 2-15cm tall, infrequent on dry limestone or grassy light soils. **Flowers** Apr-Jun, tiny 2mm across, sharp blue; flower-tube shorter than calyx; **leaves** oval, hairy, mainly in ground rosette.

CHANGING FORGET-ME-NOT *Myosotis discolour*

Scarce hairy annual on open grassland or disturbed ground, 8-20cm tall. **Flowers** May-Jun, tiny 2mm across, open yellow then turn blue; flower tube twice length of calyx; **leaves** oval, hairy.

WATER FORGET-ME-NOT
M. scorpioides
Frequent creeping perennial on watersides; upright flowering stems to 30cm and submerged runners. **Flowers** Jun-Oct 8-10mm; calyx with triangular lobes; **leaves** broad oblong.

forget-me-nots on wetland

PALE FORGET-ME-NOT
M. stolonifera
Rare post-glacial confined to a few northern streams. Mostly prostrate stems to 30cm with runners. **Flowers** Jun-Aug, 5mm, very pale blue, buds cream; hairs appressed; **leaves** spoon-shaped, bluish green.

TUFTED FORGET-ME-NOT
M. laxa
Often grows with water forget-me-not but has no creeping runners. Common in marsh or stream away from the high moors. **Flowers** May-Aug, only 4-5mm across; calyx with long narrow pointed lobes, petals rounded; <u>hairs appressed</u> to stems.

CREEPING FORGET-ME-NOT
M. secunda
Occasional rhizomatous annual or perennial, mainly upland in marsh and peat bogs. **Flowers** May-Aug, greyish blue 6-8mm across; calyx teeth long, pointed narrow; <u>hairs spreading on lower stems</u>; petals slightly notched; **leaves** oval, greyish.

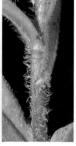

Comfreys *Symphytum spp* are familiar robust roadside perennials with large coarse, pointed, oval leaves and coils of bell-shaped flowers, white, yellowish, pink, blue or mauve.

COMMON COMFREY
Symphytum officinale

Despite its name, this native species is very uncommon in this area, occurring more frequently in southern UK. Prefers moist ground and river banks. **Flowers** May-Jul, cream or dull mauve on stems to 1.5m tall; <u>upper stems are prominently winged</u> between leaf nodes.

RUSSIAN COMFREY
Symphytum x uplandicum

Introduced and cultivated as a forage plant from 1870, now commonly naturalised on roadsides and wasteland. It is a hybrid between *S.officinale* and *S. asperum* from Eastern Europe. **Flowers** Jun-Aug, purple to blue on stems to 1.5m; <u>upper stems have little or no wings</u> between nodes.

CREEPING COMFREY
S. grandiflorum
Early-flowering low patch-forming plant, short to 20cm. **Flowers** Mar-Sep, reddish in bud, turn to cream; sepal teeth long, narrow. Introduced early C20th as garden ground cover, has spread to a few verges near habitation.

HOUNDSTONGUE
Cynoglossum officinale

BSBI

TUBEROUS COMFREY
S. tuberosum
Native plant in Scottish Lowlands, locally rare as a garden escape. Spreads far by fleshy rhizomes. Middle leaves largest on unwinged stems up to 60cm. **Flowers** May-Jun, cream or pale yellow; sepal teeth long, pointed, curl back.

WHITE COMFREY
S. orientale
Introduced in C18th for gardens, is established on a few hedge-banks near habitation. Grows to 70cm. **Flowers** pure white appear early April onwards; sepal teeth short and blunt; **leaves** rounded, softly downy; stems unwinged.

Lowland biennial, up to 60 cm, rare on limey bare or grassy ground, smells of mice. **Flowers** maroon, 6-10mm May-Aug; **leaves** greyish, downy, wavy-edged; nutlets small with hooked bristles to aid animal dispersion.

DEAD-NETTLE FAMILY *LAMIACEAE*

Square-stemmed herbs, mostly aromatic with opposite leaves, flowers lipped or bell-shaped in whorls.

HEDGE WOUNDWORT *Stachys sylvatica*

Coarse, strong-smelling common perennial with bristly stems erect to 1m; patch-forming in semi-shady damp hedgebanks, wood edge and scrub. **Flowers** Jun-Sep, with hooded upper lip, lobed lower lip, 15mm, beetroot-purple, blotched white; 5 bristly sepal teeth; loose whorls on terminal spike; **leaves** stalked, pointed oval, toothed.

MARSH WOUNDWORT *Stachys palustris*

Uncommon perennial on rough, marshy ground, streamside or field edge. Faint-smelling, hairy, erect stems to 1m in small groups. **Flowers** Jun-Sep, with hooded upper lip, lobed lower lip, c15mm, pink/mauve with white marks; 5 bristly calyx teeth; **leaves** mostly stalkless, lanceolate, toothed.

Stachys x ambigua, an infrequent hybrid between the above 2 species, shows intermediate features.

FIELD WOUNDWORT
Stachys arvensis

Infrequent colonial annual on disturbed ground with non-calcareous soil. Hairy flowering stems erect to 25cm. **Flowers** Apr-Nov, 6-7mm, pale pink streaked purple, hooded upper lip, lobed lower lip, few in small whorls; long sepal teeth; **leaves** blunt oval, toothed, upper unstalked.

BETONY *Stachys officinalis*

Frequent perennial in rough grassy hedge-banks, rides and fields. Hairy erect stems to 60cm. **Flowers** Jun-Sep 15mm, red/purple, slender tube projects beyond calyx, upper lip hooded, lobed lower lip; close whorls make 'square' flowerhead; **leaves** distinctive, even round toothing on blunt, narrow wedge-shaped blades.

CUT-LEAVED DEAD-NETTLE
Lamium hybridum
Scarce annual on enriched cultivated or disturbed dry ground. Similar to, and often growing with, red dead-nettle but is more slender, has deeply, unevenly toothed leaf edge and no or faint ring of hairs inside flower tube. **Flowers** Mar-Oct.

RED DEAD-NETTLE
Lamium purpureum
Common patch-forming low annual on short grassland, disturbed and bare ground. In flower most of the year. **Flowers** 6-15mm pink/purple, ring of hairs shows inside tube; calyx hairy with teeth as long as tube; **leaves** often reddish, evenly toothed, softly hairy.

HENBIT DEAD-NETTLE
Lamium amplexicaule
Short annual 5-25cm scattered on light dry soils. **Flowers** Apr-Aug, deep pink in bud, few in spaced whorls, shy to open; **leaves** in clasping pairs appear to encircle the stem, teeth ± even, rounded; lower leaves long-stalked.

WHITE DEAD-NETTLE
Lamium album
Stingless patch-forming perennial up to 60cm tall, common on verges and waste. **Flowers** Mar-Dec, white 2cm with dark ripe stamens, serrated lower lip and ring of hairs inside the tube; many packed in leafy whorls; **leaves** large, hairy, long pointed, deeply toothed, all green.

WATER MINT *Mentha aquatica*

Frequent downy, aromatic, wetland perennial, patch-forming in marsh and water-side. Erect stems to 90cm. **Flowers** Jul-Oct, mauve, tiny, packed into 2cm globular whorls along stem and at stem top; **leaves** hairy, blunt-tipped, toothed.

CORN MINT *Mentha arvensis*

Occasional on arable land. Wide spreading low perennial, sharp-scented; downy erect stems to 30cm. **Flowers** May-Oct, mauve, tiny in rounded whorls spaced up stems which have leafy tops; **leaves** hairy, shallow toothed.

SPEAR MINT *Mentha spicata*

Plants up to 90cm tall in large groups. Grown in gardens for mint sauce. **Flowers** Aug-Sep, tiny, mauve, packed into several contiguous whorls to form a terminal spike up to 8cm long; **leaves** pointed, ± hairless, shiny.

Mints often hybridise with features intermediate between parents. M.x piperata and M.x verticillata are most frequent.

ROUND-LEAVED MINT *Mentha suaveolens*

Round-leaved mint leaves are wrinkled, white-felted, appear rounded with edge teeth curled under.

Two apple-scented hairy, spreading perennials. Erect flowering stems to 90cm except where moorland sheep maintain a low leafy mat. **Flowers** Aug-Sept, tiny, pale pink, in dense, long branched spikes.

APPLE MINT *Mentha x villosa*

Apple mint leaves also wrinkled but sharply-toothed leaf edges project.

WILD BASIL
Clinopodium vulgare
Occasional hairy perennial 10-60cm in small groups on dry calcareous soils. **Flowers** Jul-Sep, 15-20mm pink, in whorls on hairy, often reddish, stem; curved bristly calyx; **leaves** hairy, oval, blunt, edge toothed.

BASIL THYME
Clinopodium acinos
Small creeping annual, rare in dry grassland or rocky ground with calcareous soil. Stems hairy, erect to 25cm. **Flowers** May-Sep, violet, blotched white 7-10mm; calyx hairy, tube pouched at base; **leaves** small oval.

COMMON CALAMINT
Clinopodium ascendens
Southern perennial, locally rare on calcareous, thin grassy or stony soils. Creeping runners produce hairy, erect flowering stems 30-60cm. **Flowers** Jul-Sep, 10-16mm, white streaked pale mauve, hairy; **leaves** softly hairy, light green.

WILD THYME   *Thymus polytrichus*
Mat-forming low evergreen perennial on richer free-draining sands, gravels and rocky ground. Frequent in patches on heathy moorland and coastal cliffs. **Flowers** May-Aug, up to 6mm across, pink/purple open flat lobes; several bunched in terminal heads; **stems** square, hairy on two sides only; **leaves** faintly-scented, small oval pairs.

GROUND-IVY   *Glechoma hederaceae*
Carpeting or trailing low, hairy perennial common and spreading on fertile soils, on banks and wood edge. **Flowers** Mar-May, blue/violet (occasionally pink), 10-15mm; upper lip flat, lower lip large-lobed; flowered whorls on short erect stems; **leaves** long-stalked, almost round, blunt-toothed edge.

BUGLE *Ajuga reptans*
Common leafy perennial in damp woods with non-calcareous soils. Spreads by leafy rooting runners. Flowering stems erect to 30cm, hairy on 2 sides. **Flowers** Apr-Jun, strong blue c.15mm, lower lip streaked white; leafy open whorls form short terminal spikes; **leaves** hairless, shiny green/bronze.

SELFHEAL *Prunella vulgaris*
Common spreading, slightly hairy perennial in meadows, woods, lawns and grassy waste. Square erect flowering stems to 30cm with oblong heads usually with several empty bronze, hairy calyx remains. **Flowers** Jun-Oct, violet, 10-14mm; **leaves** dull green oval, downy.

GYPSYWORT
Lycopus europaeus
Infrequent patch-forming perennial to 1m tall in habitats beside fresh water away from the hills. **Flowers** Jun-Sep, only 3-5mm, with 4 equal lobes, white with purple marks; **leaves** deeply toothed.

WILD CLARY
Salvia verbenaca
Aromatic perennial, rare north of the Wash, clings to a rocky site at *Scarborough Castle*. Tough stems to 80cm. **Flowers** Jun-Aug, dusky blue; long white hairs on calyx; **leaves** toothed, greyish.

BLACK HOREHOUND *Ballota nigra*
Strong-smelling hairy perennial, occasional in
nutrient-rich soils on waysides; groups of stems 40-
80cm tall. **Flowers** Jun-Oct, 10-18mm, hairy all over,
dull purple, hooded upper lip, 4-lobed lower lip;
numerous in whorled spikes; **leaves** rough, stalked,
coarse-toothed.

MARJORAM *Origanum vulgare*
Frequent on dry, calcareous banks, verges, scrub.
Downy perennial, forms large clumps 60cm high.
Flowers Jul-Sep, mauve,
darker in bud, 6-8mm, 2
lipped, prominent projecting
stamens; **leaves** aromatic.

SKULLCAP *Scutellaria galericulata*
Short wetland perennial, often secreted amongst
larger plants. Erect stems to 50cm from creeping
rhizomes. **Flowers** Jun-Sep,
10-20mm, strong blue in
pairs, tube curved, much
longer than calyx; flowers
soon drop; **leaves** pointed,
toothed, short-stalked.

WOOD SAGE *Teucrium scorodonia*
Downy erect perennial, stems 15-60cm; small
colonies on more acid dry soils, woods, heaths, rail
ballast, hedgerows. **Flowers** Jul-Sep, yellow,
stamens red; long cup-shaped
lower lip; flowers in pairs form
one-sided spike; **leaves** large,
pointed, wrinkled, yellowish
green.

COMMON HEMP-NETTLE *Galeopsis tetrahit*

Unobtrusive branched leafy annual, widespread on verges and in scrub woodland. Stems 10-80cm, bristly with sticky hairs, swollen at leaf nodes. **Flowers** Jul-Sep, 13-20mm, pink or cream; whorls spaced on stems; **leaves** long, oval, pointed, coarse-toothed, hairy.

BIFID HEMP-NETTLE
Galeopsis bifida is like common hemp-nettle but flowers have a cleft lower lip and are usually more darkly coloured.

RED HEMP-NETTLE *Galeopsis angustifolia*

Nationally rare downy annual of arable land, survives locally in an old limestone quarry. Stems to 60cm, scarcely swollen at nodes. **Flowers** Jul-Oct, 15-25mm, rosy/purple with white on lower lip; **leaves** narrow lanceolate.

LARGE HEMP-NETTLE *Galeopsis speciosa*

Formerly a frequent colourful annual in arable fields with peaty soils, now very scarce. Stems erect to 1m, bristly. **Flowers** Jul-Sep, 20-45mm, yellow wings and top petal, purple and orange-blotched lip; **leaves** hairy.

YELLOW ARCHANGEL *Lamiastrum galeobdolon*

Occasional in ancient woodland or scrub, patch-forming perennial to 60cm tall. **Flowers** Apr-Jun, 17-21mm, yellow with orange honey guides. Garden escapes have silver-blotched **leaves**.

PLANTAIN FAMILY PLANTAGINACEAE

Flowers tiny, 4-petalled with numerous projecting stamens, packed into terminal spikes on unbranched stems; leaves parallel-veined, shape important for identification.

RIBWORT PLANTAIN *Plantago lanceolata*
Widespread, softly hairy perennial found in a variety of habitats including sea cliffs, pastures, riverbanks, road verges and stone outcrops; avoids only very acidic soils. **Flowers** Apr-Oct, packed on stubby spikes, greenish with white stamens; stalks deeply furrowed 10-40cm; **leaves** long lanceolate, strongly-veined, short-stalked.

GREATER PLANTAIN *Plantago major*
Low perennial common on trampled paths, waysides. **Flowers** Jun-Oct, dull white, stamens yellowish, stems 10-15cm; **leaves** broad, long-stalked, hairless, mostly flat.

SEA PLANTAIN *Plantago maritima*
Plentiful on coastal cliffs, non-tidal upper shore, saltmarsh. **Flowers** Jun-Sep, tiny, dull white with yellowish stamens, on stems to 30cm; **leaves** fleshy, hairless, narrow.

HOARY PLANTAIN *Plantago media*
Fragrant downy perennial, frequent in small groups on limestone grassland and boulder clay on coastal cliffs. **Flowers** May-Aug, in oblong spikes, white with pink stamens; flower stalks unfurrowed 4-6cm; **leaves** broad oval, covered with soft hairs, appear greyish.

BUCK'S-HORN PLANTAIN *Plantago coronopus*
Downy low coastal biennial, also occasionally on grazed salt-sprayed verges. **Flowers** May-Jul, in short spike, buff with pale yellow stamens; **leaves** have short linear segments resembling tiny deer antlers.

FIGWORT FAMILY *SCROPHULARIACEAE*

Flowers vary widely but all have a 2-lobed ovary and fruit capsule with 2 many-seeded cells - this distinguishes them from rather similar *Lamiaceae* plants which have a 4-lobed ovary and fruit of 4 single-seeded nutlets.

COMMON FIGWORT *Scrophularia nodosa*

WATER FIGWORT *Scrophularia auriculata*

Leafy perennials to 2m tall. **Flowers** Jun-Sep, c.10mm, with 2 red/brown upper and 3 green lower lobes; 5 sepals.

Frequent on damp fertile soils, usually in light shade. Square stems to 1m without wings, hairless, branched; **leaves** opposite, short-stalked, pointed, coarsely toothed.

Prefers stream edge, marsh, wet woodland. Stems square with 4 wings; **leaves** round ended, bluntly toothed and usually have a pair of small leaflets at base; sepals white-edged.

GREAT MULLEIN *Verbascum thapsus*

DARK MULLEIN *Verbascum nigrum*

Stout white-woolly biennial to 2m tall. Infrequent in open scrub, railway banks, quarries on well-drained soils. **Flowers** Jun-Aug, 5-30mm, in dense terminal spikes; stamens yellow; **leaves** white felted, broad oval, stalk wings continue down main stem.

Resembles great mullein but has a green, hairy (not woolly) angled stem; **Flowers** Jun-Sep, stamen stalks covered with dense purple hairs; **leaves** dark green crinkled, not woolly. North of its natural range but a few garden escapes persist. *Hartoft.*

FOXGLOVE
Digitalis purpurea

Colourful (rarely white) biennial to 2m tall, often in large open spreads. Common in forest clearings, on hedgebanks, heath and waste land with acidic soil. **Flowers** Jun-Aug, c.4cm long open bell has extended lower lip, pink with white-circled black dots inside; **leaves** large oval, downy wrinkled.

COW-WHEAT *Melampyrum pratense*

Semi-parasitic patch-forming annual, infrequent on upland heaths, moors, in open deciduous woodland on acidic soils. Hairless erect stems to 60cm. **Flowers** May-Sep, yellow, 10-18mm, 2-lipped (lower longer, flat); in pairs on same side of stem; **leaves** long, narrow, pointed oval, in pairs.

YELLOW-RATTLE *Rhinanthus minor*

Occasional semi-parasitic annual on verges, fields, cliffs. Erect stems to 50cm, black-spotted. **Flowers** May-Aug, 12-15mm yellow, 2 violet teeth on upper lip, convex lower lip; **leaves** opposite, in pairs, stalkless, narrow lanceolate, toothed; seeds rattle inside papery, inflated calyx when ripe.

RED BARTSIA *Odontites vernus*

Reddish, branched, downy annual, erect to 50cm. In small groups on tracks and in short grassy places. **Flowers** Jun-Sep, 8-10mm, dusky pink, slightly hooded upper lip, 3-lobed lower lip; several on slender, leafy spike; **leaves** small narrow lanceolate, scarcely toothed, stalkless opposite pairs.

MONKEYFLOWERS *Mimulus spp*
Showy, mainly waterside, plants were introduced in the early C18th; some have hybridised and created large spreads along streams and riversides. Leafy perennials; yellow flowers, 2 upper and 3 lower flat lobes.

MONKEYFLOWER
M.guttatus
Flowers 3-4cm, yellow with red-spotted throat; **leaves** broad, toothed, clasp the stem. Infrequent in ponds, ditches; also planted in amenity schemes.

HYBRID MONKEYFLOWER
M x robertsii
Flowers 2.5-4cm, deep yellow, each lobe blotched red; anthers usually without pollen but spreads from stem fragments. More a plant of upland riversides, scarce in this area.

MUSK *M.moschatus*
Introduced for its fragrance which has since been lost; locally very uncommon; sticky, downy small plant up to 40cm. **Flowers** pale yellow unspotted, only 1-2cm across; **leaves** pale, sticky hairy.

LOUSEWORT *Pedicularis sylvatica*   **MARSH LOUSEWORT** *Pedicularis palustris*

A short semi-parasitic perennial, common on damp acidic heaths and boggy moors. Many lax stems sprawl to 25cm. **Flowers** Apr-Jul, pink/purple; erect upper lip hooded with 2 teeth; lower lip lobed; inflated and ribbed hairless calyx; **leaves** appear 'frilly' with serrate-edged small leaflets.

Annual or biennial, less frequent and flowers later than common lousewort; grows in more enriched marshland. Single stem upright to 60cm, branched at base. **Flowers** May-Sep, pink/purple, upper lip with 4 teeth; calyx downy; **leaves** deeply and evenly lobed.

EYEBRIGHT *Euphrasia sp*

Short, branched, semi-parasitic annual, variable with numerous microspecies. Common on short grassland, heath. **Flowers** Jul-Sep, 4-11mm, white (or mauve) with purple and yellow markings; 2-lipped, both lips lobed giving 'frilly' appearance; **leaves** small oval, sharply serrate-edged.

FAIRY FOXGLOVE *Erinus alpinus*

Small, short-lived garden annual; spread to the wild from its prolific seeding. Grows on sunny limestone-wall crevices and gravel. **Flowers** May-Oct, 4-10mm, soft mauve; long tube opens to 5 notched unequal petals; **leaves** small oval, slightly crenate-edged.
Helmsley Castle

SMALL TOADFLAX *Chaenorhinum minus*

Low-growing small hairy annual, occasional in lime-rich soils; appears in spring on arable land, limestone walls, dry bare ground and rail ballast. **Flowers** Jun-Oct, 6-9mm, pale purple and cream with short spur; stems to 25 cm; **leaves** small, greyish, slender oval.

IVY-LEAVED TOADFLAX *Cymbalaria muralis*

Introduced for gardens in the C16th, this small creeping plant is well established, trailing over old walls and stony ground, often near villages. **Flowers** on long slender stalks Apr-Dec, 9-15mm, mauve touched with yellow, short spur; **leaves** small ivy-leaf shaped, often bronze-tinted.

Speedwells have small, blue or lilac, flat, open flowers with 2 protruding stamens and 4 petals - usually 2 matching at the sides, topmost larger and lowest smaller; 14 local species adapted to differing habitats.

BROOKLIME *Veronica beccabunga*

Common robust perennial, forms dense mats in shallow streams, ponds, marshes; thick, hairless, often red, rooting stems. **Flowers** May-Sep, 7-8mm, deep blue; **leaves** shiny, hairless, shallow-toothed oval.

MARSH SPEEDWELL *Veronica scutellata*

Infrequent in flushes, bogs, marshes; slender, much-branched perennial to15cm. **Flowers** Jun-Aug, 5-6mm, pale blue/ white, few on short open spikes; **leaves** short, narrow, yellow/green or bronze.

BLUE WATER SPEEDWELL *Veronica anagallis-aquatica*

Uncommon branched waterside perennial, erect to 50cm in ponds, ditches. **Flowers** Jun-Aug, 5-10mm, pale blue, numerous in long terminal upright spikes; **leaves** long, lanceolate, mostly unstalked.

PINK WATER SPEEDWELL *Veronica catenata*

Locally rare annual in shallow pondside or mud. Erect to 40cm, wide-spreading side branches. **Flowers** Jun-Aug, pink 3-5mm; **leaves** long, narrow; fruit stalks mostly at right-angles to main stem.

COMMON FIELD SPEEDWELL
Veronica persica

Low, hairy, spreading annual abundant on arable land. **Flowers** Jan-Dec, 8-12mm, <u>blue with pale lower petal,</u> on long stalks; **leaves** pea-green, almost rounded, toothed, hairy below; fruit has 2 widely divergent lobes above spreading calyx.

GREY FIELD SPEEDWELL
Veronica polita

Flowers 4-8mm, <u>petals all bright blue</u>; leaves grey/green; fruit with upright, not spreading, calyx lobes.

Both grey and green field speedwells were C18th introduced annuals, now naturalised and scattered in fields and gardens but not common. Smaller flowers, but similar in growth form and habitat to common field speedwell.

GREEN FIELD SPEEDWELL
Veronica agrestis

Flowers 4-8mm, <u>pale blue, lower petal white</u>; short flower stalks; **leaves** pale green; erect fruit lobes.

IVY-LEAVED SPEEDWELL
Veronica hederifolia

Early low-growing hairy annual, spreads far on hedgebanks, churchyards, waysides. **Flowers** Apr-May, only 4-6mm with lilac petals in the widespread ssp *lucorum;* 6-9mm with blue petals in the less frequent ssp *hederifolia*; **leaves** light green, ivy-shaped.

SLENDER SPEEDWELL
Veronica filiformis

Introduced from Turkey for gardens, now frequent in the wild where it spreads from mown fragments. Mat-forming low perennial, common in churchyards, on lawns and verges. **Flowers** Apr-Jun, 8-15mm, blue/mauve with white lower petal, long flower-stalks; **leaves** kidney-shape, wavy-edged, light green.

GERMANDER SPEEDWELL
Veronica chamaedrys

Common perennial in short grassy places; sprawling, patch-forming; stems reddish with 2 distinct lines of hairs. **Flowers** Mar-Jul, 8-12mm, sharp blue with white eye (also pale blue variant), on short stalks; **leaves** hairy, blunt-toothed.

WALL SPEEDWELL
Veronica arvensis

Tiny-flowered spreading, downy annual 5-20cm tall, frequent in dry soils, on waste, gravel tracks, walls, heaths. **Flowers** Mar-Oct, deep blue c.4mm, secreted in leafy stem tops; **leaves** dark green, small, toothed.

WOOD SPEEDWELL
Veronica montana

Short, branched perennial, scattered in open old woodland and shady hedgebanks. Stems to 30cm, hairy all round. **Flowers** Apr-Jul, 8-10mm, pale lilac/blue on long stalks; **leaves** large, yellow/green, coarse-toothed.

HEATH SPEEDWELL
Veronica officinalis

Hairy, creeping, mat-forming perennial frequent on well-drained heath and more acid grassy banks. **Flowers** May-Aug, 6-9mm, pale lilac, short-stalked, many in terminal spikes; **leaves** small, hairy, broad oval, shallow-toothed.

THYME-LEAVED SPEEDWELL
Veronica serpylifolia

Frequent on woodland rides, grassy heaths, bare ground; hairless, creeping perennial with slender erect stems 5-20cm. **Flowers** Apr-Oct, on leafy upper stems, 5-6mm, pale blue/white with dark veins; **leaves** small neat oval, shiny.

COMMON TOADFLAX
Linaria vulgaris
Infrequent perennial on verges, field edge, grassy banks with calcareous soil. **Flowers** Jun-Oct, yellow and orange with spur, in terminal spikes on erect downy stems to 80cm tall; **leaves** numerous, narrow strap-shaped, appear greyish with fine hairs.

PURPLE TOADFLAX
Linaria purpurea
Colourful garden escape occasional on verges, waste ground. Waving flowered spikes up to 1m tall. **Flowers** Jun-Sep, 7-15mm, purple or pink, with curved spur; **leaves** narrow strap-shaped, greyish.

SHARP-LEAVED FLUELLEN *Kickxia elatine*
Low trailing slender annual on calcareous or sandy arable land. A native of southern Europe, long associated with cornfields in southern UK, it was discovered in a field near Seamer in 2000. This is thought to be its most northerly site. **Flowers** Jul-Oct, 7-9mm, tiny purple 2-lobed upper lip, yellow 3-lobed lower lip, small straight spur; **leaves** arrow-shaped, hairy.

BIRD'S-NEST FAMILY MONOTROPACEAE

YELLOW BIRD'S-NEST *Monotropa hypopitys*
Rare perennial, lacks green chlorophyll, saprophytic on decaying vegetation. **Flowers** Jun-Aug, small bell-shaped, pale yellow, grouped at the top of scaly stems 8-20cm tall, drooping in flower, erect in fruit.

Dalby Forest

BROOMRAPE FAMILY *OROBANCHACEAE*

KNAPWEED BROOMRAPE *Orobanche elatior*

Rare at its northern UK limit. Buff perennial, parasitic on greater knapweed, lacks any green colouring. **Flowers** Jun-Jul, 18-25mm, have crinkly-edged lobes around yellow style and stamens; thick scaly stem erect 30-70cm. *Slingsby, Crossgates.*

TOOTHWORT *Lathraea squamaria*

Flesh-pink perennial, also known as Dead Man's Fingers. Uncommon in deciduous woods, scrub, verges. Lacks green chlorophyll; parasitic, usually on hazel, ash or elm. **Flowers** Apr-May, tubular in one-sided spike at the top of thick, scaly stem 8-30cm.

BLADDERWORT FAMILY *LENTIBULARIACEAE*

COMMON BUTTERWORT *Pinguicula vulgaris*

Northern insectivorous perennial, occasional in bogs, flushes, seeping rock crevices. **Flowers** May-Jul, blue/violet, pointed spur, 14-22mm. solitary on c.12cm stems; **leaves** light yellow/green, inrolled margins; sticky to ensnare insects.

BLADDERWORT *Utricularia agg.*

Rare insectivorous, underwater, rootless perennial. **Flowers** Jul-Aug, 12-18mm, erratic flowering in *Gilling Lake*; **leaves** submerged; finely-divided, have small bladders which trap insects.

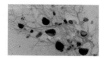

BELLFLOWER FAMILY *CAMPANULACEAE*

Open bell or wheel-shaped flowers with 5 similar petal lobes; leaves undivided, alternate. Fruit a capsule.

GIANT BELLFLOWER *Campanula latifolia*

Large showy perennial, occasional in non-acidic damp woodland or hedge banks. Stems bluntly angular, to 1m or more tall, in colonies. **Flowers** Jul-Aug, 40-50mm diam, light blue or mauve bells, numerous on leafy upper stems; calyx with pointed lobes; **leaves** broad, toothed, pointed.

HAREBELL *Campanula rotundifolia*

Common rhizomatous perennial, spreads in infertile soils on heath, railsides, verges. Slender, waving stems to 40cm. **Flowers** Jul-Sep, delicate, hanging bells, soft mauve/blue, 10-20mm; **leaves** rounded, crenate-edged, long-stalked from the base, soon die back; stem leaves narrow, linear, persist.

CLUSTERED BELLFLOWER *Campanula glomerata*

As a native perennial, rare in a few sheltered, more calcareous grassy sites; as a garden escape, occasional on verges. **Flowers** Jun-Oct, deep purple bells 12-25mm, clustered on short, stiff, hairy, often reddish stalks; **leaves** pointed oval, stalked at base, upper sessile.

VENUS'S LOOKING-GLASS *Legousia hybrida*

Rare in arable fields on calcareous soils. Hairy annual 5-20cm. **Flowers** May-Aug, 5-lobed wheel shape c.7mm across; blue/purple when open, pale blue when petals closed; shy to open in dull weather; **leaves** wavy-edged oval, mainly on stem; fruit triangular, long, tube-like.

BEDSTRAW FAMILY   *RUBIACEAE*

Plants with whorls of narrow, pointed leaves; flowers with 4 (or 5) petals, tiny or no sepals, 4 stamens, 2 styles.

CLEAVERS or GOOSEGRASS   *Galium aparine*
Common clinging annual on hedges, waysides, waste, clambers over other vegetation; rough stems to 3m have large backward-pointing prickles. **Flowers** May-Sep, greenish white, only 2mm, in small clusters; whorls of 6-8 **leaves** with backward-pointing edge prickles, strong end-point; fruit with hooked bristles.

HEDGE BEDSTRAW   *Galium mollugo*
Infrequent on hedge banks, railside, wood edge; robust, shiny green perennial, upright or trailing up to 1m. **Flowers** Jun-Aug, white, 3-4mm, in large open bunches; **leaves** 6-8 in a whorl, forward-pointing edge prickles, short end-point.

HEATH BEDSTRAW   *Galium saxatile*
Low dense carpeting perennial, common on acidic heath, grassy waste. **Flowers** Jun-Aug, white, only 3mm on short upright stems; **leaves** dull green small, have forward-pointing edge prickles, short end-point.

MARSH BEDSTRAW
Galium palustre
Clambering hairless perennial, frequent in marshes. Stems have no prickles. **Flowers** Jun-Aug, white, 3-4mm in wide sprays; **leaves** 4-5 per whorl, forward-pointing edge prickles, no end points.

FEN BEDSTRAW   *Galium uliginosum*
Similar to marsh bedstraw, but prefers lime-rich marsh. Stem rough on the angles with backward-pointing prickles. **Flowers** in narrow sprays; **leaves** 5-8 per whorl, backward-pointing edge prickles, sharp end point.

CROSSWORT *Cruciata laevipes*

Fragrant perennial, common in deep, well-drained soil on hedge banks, waysides. Slender stems 15-60cm tall, usually in colonies. **Flowers** May-Jun, yellow, 2-3mm, in dense whorled clusters; **leaves** yellow/green, 3-veined, hairy, 4 in a whorl.

LADY'S BEDSTRAW *Galium verum*

Common on verges, waysides, old quarries. Creeping stems create large groups of erect, hairless stems 15-60cm tall. **Flowers** Jul-Aug, golden yellow, 2-3mm, in leafy clusters; **leaves** dark green, one-veined, linear, hairless, with end-point.

WOODRUFF *Galium odoratum*

Frequent spreads in woodland and shady hedge banks on damp soils. Stems, 15-30cm. **Flowers** May-Jun, 4-6mm, white, tube opens to 4 pointed lobes; **leaves** in whorls, dark, shiny green; forward-pointing edge prickles and end-point; fruit round, covered with hooked bristles.

FIELD MADDER *Sherardia arvensis*

Occasional in dry arable fields, short grassland, cliffs. Hairless, prostrate annual, sprawls to 40cm. **Flowers** Jun-Sep, mauve, 4-petalled, 3-5mm, grouped in small, leafy heads; **leaves** in whorls of 4-6, with backward-pointing prickles and end-point on leaflets.

HONEYSUCKLE FAMILY *CAPRIFOLIACEAE*

HONEYSUCKLE *Lonicera periclymenum*
Widespread in woods and hedges away from high moor and wetland.
Deciduous perennial; twining woody stems to 6m. **Flowers** Jun-Sep,
funnel-shaped with long tube and projecting stamens; very fragrant;
leaves dark green above, glaucous beneath; fruit a red berry.

ELDER *Sambucus nigra*
Common deciduous large bush in hedgerows, woods and waysides. **Flowers** May-Aug, small, creamy white and aromatic,
grouped in flat heads; **leaves** pinnate, leaflets dark green, toothed;
fruit juicy edible black berries hang in bunches on red stalks.

GUELDER-ROSE *Viburnum opulus*
Deciduous large shrub to 4m, frequent on damp, limey hedgebanks
and scrub. **Flowerhead** Jun-Jul, 5-10cm, has ring of large 5-
petalled sterile flowers around fertile small inner ones; **leaves** broad
palmate with irregularly toothed lobes; **fruit** green berry turns red.

SNOWBERRY *Symphoricarpos albus*
Introduced suckering shrub, occasionally forms dense thickets up to
2m tall in hedgerow, wood edge and scrub. **Flowers** Jun-Sep, bell-
shaped, pink 5-8mm; prominent white berries; **leaves** oval.

VALERIAN FAMILY VALERIANACEAE

Herbs with 5-lobed tubular flowers, either pouched or spurred; 1 or 3 stamens.

MARSH VALERIAN
Valeriana dioica
Frequent dioecious perennial in marsh, alder carr. Stems erect to 40cm. Flowerheads pale pink, dense bunches of female **flowers** 1-2mm or male 3-5mm May-Jun; **leaves** long-stalked and spoon-shaped at base; pinnate leaves on stem.

COMMON VALERIAN
Valeriana officinalis
Common tall wetland perennial in wet woods, ditches, marshes. Stems erect to 2m. **Flowers** 4-5mm, pale pink, in domed heads Jun-Aug; **leaves** sessile on stem, stalked below, all with toothed leaflets.

RED VALERIAN
Centranthus ruber
Garden introduction naturalised on sea cliffs, walls. Bushy almost succulent, greyish invasive perennial 30-80cm. **Flowers** pink or white tubes with 5 open lobes, 5mm across, massed in large heads May-Sep; **leaves** grey/green oval, prominent central vein.

COMMON CORNSALAD *Valerianella locusta*
Unusual short annual in cultivated ground, gravel and rail ballast. Edible, also known as lamb's lettuce. Multi-forked branches to 30cm. **Flowers** Apr-Jun, 1-2mm, pale blue/mauve; **leaves** long spoon-shaped; **nutlet** globular, scarcely grooved.

NARROW-FRUITED CORNSALAD
Valerianella dentata
Locally rare in lime-rich arable fields. **Flowers** Jun-Aug,1-2mm, pale pink; **leaves** narrow, often with single edge tooth; **nutlet** pear-shaped with 2 distinct ribs.

TEASEL FAMILY DIPSACACEAE

WILD TEASEL *Dipsacus fullonum*
Prickly biennial, occasional in rough grassy places and waste. Ridged, spiny stem to 2m tall, arises in the second year; **leaves** prickly in ground rosette which soon dies back, stem leaves with cupped clasping base. **Flowerhead** Jul-Aug, oval 3-8cm long, surrounded by long thin spiny bracts; florets small pink/purple, shorter than encasing, spiny bracts.

FIELD SCABIOUS *Knautia arvensis*
Frequent on non-acidic soils, roadsides, field edge. Robust roughly hairy perennial to 1m tall. **Flowerhead** Jun-Oct, mauve/blue 3-4cm across, slightly domed; edge florets larger; stamens pink; bracts beneath flowerhead in 2 unequal rows; **leaves** both large simple oval and deeply lobed; all hairy, toothed.

DEVIL'S-BIT SCABIOUS *Succisa pratensis*
Occasional in more acidic soils on grassland, wood, scrub, cliffs, heath. Sparsely hairy branched perennial erect to 1m. **Flowerheads** Jun-Oct, deep mauve, domed, c.2cm across; all florets similar size; stamens pink or purple; bracts beneath flowerhead various lengths; **leaves** not divided, lanceolate, scarcely toothed.

SMALL SCABIOUS *Scabiosa columbaria*
Sparse in limestone grassland and verges, old quarries. Slightly hairy perennial, erect to 15-70cm. **Flowerheads** Jul-Sep, blue/mauve 2-3cm across; edge florets larger; thin black bristles show between unequal bracts beneath flowerhead; **leaves** on upper stems have narrow lobes, lower leaves lobed with large oval end leaflet, all softly hairy.

DAISY FAMILY ASTERACEAE

A large group of plants, also known as composites from the close cluster of separate flowers in a single head. Individual flowers *(florets)* are small with petals joined into a tube; this may open into 5 tiny teeth *(tubular or disc florets)* or have a single petal-like extension *(strap or ray florets)*. All florets rise in a dense flowerhead from a circular disc *(receptacle)* at the end of a stem. Beneath the receptacle usually lie green calyx-like bracts whose shape helps with plant identification. Fruits frequently have a parachute of fine hairs *(pappus)* to aid wind dispersal; others have curled bristles to help seed dispersal by animals.

BUTTERBUR *Petasites hybridus*

Covers extensive patches often on alluvial soil in marshes, meadows, road and stream sides. Creeping perennial ± dioecious with stout fleshy stems. **Leaves** emerge as flowers fade, then enlarge to >1m across; **flowerheads** Mar-May, male 7-12cm long with reddish-pink tubular florets; female plants separate and rare.

WINTER HELIOTROPE *Petasites fragrans*

Introduced in 1806, continues to spread on verges and in churchyards. Extensive patch-forming early-flowering perennial with strong vanilla fragrance. Thick hollow hairy flower-stems erect to 30cm with small 'shaving-brush' **flowerheads** Dec-Mar, white and purple; **leaves** almost circular, cordate, bright green.

MOUNTAIN EVERLASTING
Antennaria dioica

Mountain plant on thin, heathy ground, locally very rare. Dioecious, short, white-woolly perennial; rooting runners form small groups of erect flowering stems 5-20cm. **Flowerheads** Jun-Jul, male 6mm pink, tipped white; female 12mm woolly, pink, on separate plants; **leaves** small oval, green above, white-woolly below.

COMMON KNAPWEED *Centaurea nigra*

Also known as hardheads; common on verges, banks, sea cliffs.. Variable, coarse perennial; branched 15-60cm stems stiff, grooved, dull greyish green. **Flowerheads** Jul-Sep, solitary, 2-4cm across; florets red/purple; buff-edged dark bracts surround hard globular receptacle; **leaves** lanceolate, lobed lower down, clasping.

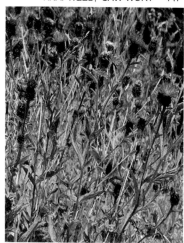

GREATER KNAPWEED
Centaurea scabiosa

Occasional on dry calcareous soils, fieldside, wood edge, verges. Hairy perennial, has erect grooved stems to 1m. **Flowerheads** Jul-Sep, 3-6cm across, flat with fringe of finely-split outer ray florets, spreading and drooping; inner florets short-rayed, all red/purple; receptacle bracts green, dark-edged; **leaves** large, deeply-lobed.

SAW-WORT *Serratula tinctoria*

Rare in lime-rich grassland, quarries, scrub. Slender, hairless perennial. Grooved stems erect to 80cm. **Flowerheads** Jul-Sep, up to 2cm long; small brush-like head of red/purple, ± erect florets; appressed, white-edged purple bracts enclose narrow, oblong receptacle; **leaves** slender, pointed, with narrow leaflets all edged with fine saw-like teeth, dark green.

CREEPING THISTLE *Cirsium arvense*

Very common in rough grassy places and cultivated land. Much-branched creeping perennial up to 1m tall; stems furrowed, not winged, mostly without spines. **Flowerheads** Jun-Oct, fragrant, mauve, 1cm across and up to 1.5cm long, in open clusters; receptacle bracts purplish, spine-tipped; **leaves** spiny.

SPEAR THISTLE *Cirsium vulgare*

Widespread in a range of grassy and bare habitats. Large bushy, very spiny biennial. Stems to 1.5m tall, cottony, spiny wings. **Flowerheads** Jul-Oct, 2-3cm across; brush of pink/purple florets above large oval receptacle covered with yellow-tipped, green spines; **leaves** lobed with long, stout spines.

MARSH THISTLE *Cirsium palustre*

Large, open-branched, purplish biennial common in damp grassland, marshes, heath. Continuously spiny-winged, hairy stems up to 2.5m tall. **Flowerheads** Jun-Oct, brush-like, in tight clusters; florets purple (or white); oval receptacle with green/purple bracts; **leaves** long, narrow, shiny, wavy-edged with purplish spines.

MILK THISTLE *Silybum marianum* Very rare on thin grassland. Stout, spineless, white-woolly stems up to 1m tall; solitary **flowers** Jun-Aug, 40-50mm, have long, sharp, yellow-tipped spines; white-veined spiny leaves.

WOOLLY THISTLE *Cirsium eriophorum*

Rare on calcareous scrub. Robust biennial, erect stems up to 2m, round, cottony, not spiny. **Flowerheads** Jul-Sep, large solitary, 4-7cm across; purple florets above round spiny receptacle, densely entwined with white wool; **leaves** long, green above, white cottony below; strongly-spined lobes point in 3 directions.

MEADOW THISTLE *Cirsium dissectum*

A southern plant of poorly-drained meadows, rare here at its northern edge. Perennial with grooved, unwinged, downy stems to 80cm and rooting runners. **Flowerheads** Jun-Aug, c.2.5cm across; florets dark red/purple; bracts cottony; **leaves** long oval, up to 3cm wide, green above, whitish but not felted below, stalked.

CARLINE THISTLE *Carlina vulgaris*

Occasional in short, calcareous grassland, rock outcrops, quarries. Spiny biennial; stiff erect flowering stems 10-60cm. **Flowerheads** Jul-Oct, 3-4cm wide; centre florets brownish, surrounded by curled or spreading straw-coloured bracts; **leaves** edged with soft spines, cottony below, clasp the stem.

DWARF THISTLE *Cirsium acaule* Low plant with spiny leaf rosette and stemless flowerhead; formerly occurred on limestone grasslands around *Rievaulx, Ellerburn and Hackness*, but has not been seen on these sites or elsewhere in recent years.

MUSK THISTLE *Carduus nutans*

Large biennial, quite frequent on grazed limestone grassland and roadside; erect stems with wavy, spiny wings except short, bare stem top. **Flowerheads** May-Aug, large, 4-6cm across, nodding, fragrant; brush-like purple ray florets above ruff of narrrow, spine-tipped, purplish bracts. **leaves** hairy, deeply lobed with long spines.

WELTED THISTLE *Carduus crispus*

Occasional on nutrient-rich waste, ditchsides or wood edge away from the moors. Erect biennial 30-120cm tall; long, thin branches with narrow, spiral, spine-edged wings. **Flowerheads** Jun-Aug, oblong, c.20mm wide, in small clusters; oval receptacle with narrow, green/purple, weakly-spined bracts; **leaves** green, narrow, spiny.

SLENDER THISTLE *Carduus tenuiflorus*

Greyish coastal species restricted to the gull-frequented *Cowbar* cliff at *Staithes*. Very spiny branched stems to 60cm. **Flowerheads** May-Aug, small, straight, only 7 0mm wide; florets pale mauve, bracts spiny, grey/green; **leaves** pale grey, downy, spiny.

LESSER BURDOCK *Arctium minus agg.*

Frequent robust and variable bushy biennial up to 2m tall and wide on wood edge, scrub, waysides. **Flowerheads** Jul-Sep, 15-30mm wide; clusters of green/purple balls of hooked, spiny bracts topped by purple florets; **leaves** large, broad oval, green above, pale beneath; lower leaf stems hollow.

BLUE SOWTHISTLE
Cicerbita macrophylla
Invasive garden
introduction, widely
established on
roadsides and
wasteland; large
swathes of 2m tall
showy plants.
Flowerheads Jul-Sep,
up to 3cm across; pale
mauve/ blue ray florets,
no disc florets; **leaves**
sticky hairy, small side
lobes, large end lobe.

SEA ASTER
Aster tripolium
Limited to fragments of
saltmarsh beside the
River Esk at *Ruswarp*
and *Whitby*. Patch-
forming, salt-tolerant,
fleshy perennial to 1m
tall. **Flowerheads** Jul-
Oct, c.2cm, mauve or
white ray florets, yellow
disc florets; **leaves**
narrow, dark green,
pointed, strong midrib.

CORNFLOWER
Centaurea cyanus
Not seen in the wild for
many decades until a
few plants appeared in
a sandy cornfield in
2005. Up to 70cm tall,
wiry branched stems.
Flowerheads Jun-
Aug, c. 3cm, blue
darkening near centre,
purple anthers; **leaves**
long narrow, covered
with grey cottony hairs.

MUGWORT
Artemisia vulgaris
Common perennial on
road verges and waste.
Branched stems to
1.5m tall, ridged, often
reddish. Spikes of
clustered small
flowerheads Jul-Sep,
with tiny yellow/brown
tubular florets encircled
by hairy greyish bracts;
leaves deeply lobed,
dark green above,
white hairy beneath.

DAISY *Bellis perennis*
Very common low rosette-forming perennial on damp lawns,

short grassland. Hairy erect
flower stems to 12cm.
Flowerheads Mar-Oct, single,
flat up to 2cm, disc florets
yellow, rays white, tipped pink;
leaves
spoon-
shaped,
basal.

OX-EYE DAISY or **DOG DAISY** *Leucanthemum vulgare*

Tall, large-flowered daisy,
plentiful on grassy roadsides,
coastal cliffs, meadows.
Groups of erect, grooved
stems to 75cm. **Flowerheads**
May-Sep, flat, 3-5cm across;
yellow disc florets surrounded
by white ray florets; **leaves**
mostly basal, round-lobed,
long-stalked and spoon-
shaped.

SHASTA DAISY *Leucanthemum x superbum* is a garden cultivar widely planted on roadsides. A fertile hybrid, it has naturalised extensively on coastal cliffs; taller and with larger flowers than ox-eye daisy.

MARSH CUDWEED
Gnaphalium uliginosum
Greyish woolly
annual, frequent on
acid damp ground
and in gateways.
Small prostrate
plants rarely 20cm
high, branched
stems **Flowerheads**
Jul-Sep, 3-4mm, in
tight clusters; **leaves**
narrow, bluish-green,
covered with dense
woolly hairs.

HEATH CUDWEED
Gnaphalium sylvaticum
Uncommon greyish perennial on
forest drives. Leafy, erect, white
woolly stems to 60cm.
Flowerheads Jul-Sept, 6mm, in leaf
axils, small brown with pale-edged
green bracts; **leaves** narrow,
pointed, woolly beneath.

© CHRIS WILSON

COMMON CUDWEED
Filago vulgaris
Infrequent short
annual on dry arable
fields, gravelly
tracks. **Flowerheads**
Jul-Aug, in small
clusters; florets tiny,
dull white, concealed
by gingery bracts;
leaves short, wavy-
edged, densely
white-woolly.

Mayweeds are widespread, persistent, sprawling, much-branched annual or perennial herbs; white-rayed outer florets, inner disc florets yellow; leaves finely divided into numerous short, linear leaflets.

CORN CHAMOMILE *Anthemis arvensis* Lowland cornfield annual on sandy or calcareous soils, appears rarely. Resembles scentless mayweed, but has all-green bracts and is slightly aromatic.

SCENTLESS MAYWEED
Tripleurospermum inodorum
Scentless; abundant in arable and disturbed ground. **Flowerheads** May-Nov, 20-45mm, centre disc solid, only slightly domed; bracts beneath flowerhead green, edged brown.

SCENTED MAYWEED
Matricaria recutita
Fragrant if bruised; occasional on lighter soils. **Flowerheads** May-Jul, 10-25mm, centre disc conical, hollow; ray florets bend backwards; flowerhead bracts green, edged white.

SEA MAYWEED
Tripleurospermum maritimum
Confined to, and plentiful on, spray zone of coastal cliffs. **Flowerheads** Jul-Sep, 30-50mm; leaves dark green, short, fleshy linear segments.

FEVERFEW *Tanacetum parthenium*
Ancient cultivated medicinal plant, frequently naturalised on walls, waysides near habitation. Low, bushy, strongly aromatic perennial; much-branched stems to 60cm. **Flowerheads** Jul-Sep, 10-20mm, flat, centre disc yellow, outer rays white; **leaves** light yellow/green, deep-lobed and round-toothed.

SHAGGY SOLDIER *Galinsoga quadriradiata*
Small opportunist annual appears from time to time in pavement cracks and bare ground, mostly in urban areas; branched and erect stems 10-75mm. **Flowerheads** Jun-Oct, 5-7mm, outer florets few, white; centre disc florets yellow; **leaves** and stems covered with white hairs.

YARROW *Achillea millefolium*

Long-flowering perennial, very common on roadside verges and in short grassy habitats. Leafy tufts with upright flowering stems 10-50cm. **Flowerheads** Jun-Dec, 40-60mm fragrant; centre disc florets buff, outer rays dull white or pink; **leaves** fern-like, long narrow, divided into dark green linear segments.

SNEEZEWORT *Achillea ptarmica*

Patch-forming in wet pasture, springs, marshes, ditches. Greyish hairy perennial. Stems branched and erect to 60cm. **Flowerheads** Jul-Sep, 10-18mm, centre disc florets greenish-grey, outer rays white; **leaves** narrow, pointed, edges finely toothed, dull green.

HEMP-AGRIMONY
Eupatorium cannabinum

Large leafy perennial, frequent in damp wood edge, waterside banks; avoids exposed uplands, more numerous towards the coast. Stems to 1.5m tall, often reddish, topped with dense trusses of **flowerheads** Jul-Sep; small pink tubular florets with long white styles and purple-tipped bracts; **leaves** have 3 or 5 large pointed toothed leaflets.

CANADIAN FLEABANE *Conyza canadensis*

Long-naturalised annual in southern UK, now quite frequent locally on light sandy disturbed ground and waste. Stems erect to 80cm. **Flowerheads** Jun-Oct, only 3-5mm across, dull white; **leaves** narrow, light green, numerous up stems.

BLUE FLEABANE *Erigeron acer*

Infrequent annual or biennial on warm, well-drained calcareous soils. Rough, hairy stems to 60cm. **Flowerheads** Jul-Sep, 12-18mm across; ray florets dull mauve, upright, disc florets yellow; **leaves** narrow lanceolate.

MEXICAN FLEABANE *Erigeron karvinskianus*

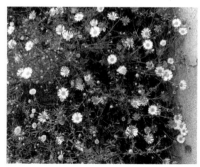

First recorded in the wild in Guernsey in 1860, has progressed northwards, reaching local sheltered sites, especially walls, in recent years. **Flowerheads** Apr-Oct, c.20mm across; ray florets deep pink to white on same plant; sprawling branched stems; **leaves** simple, pointed oval.

SEASIDE DAISY *Erigeron glaucus*
C19th garden introduction, naturalised on seafronts and walls at resorts and villages along the coast. Rare inland. Forms dense clumps 50cm tall. **Flowerheads** May-Aug, solitary, 30-40mm, with mauve ray florets and yellow disc florets. **Leaves** oval, rather fleshy.

LEPTINELLA *Cotula sp.*
A New Zealand buttonweed, first seen in NE Yorks in 2006 on *Rudlland* and *Glaisdale Riggs*. Subject to sheep and rabbit grazing, also severe weather, plants are miniature version of normal, rarely over 10cm tall. **Flowerheads** under 10mm, pale yellow, face the sun. **leaves** fleshy, deeply lobed.

Dandelion type which have all ray florets and no central disc:

dandelion, goatsbeard
hawkbit (autumn, rough, lesser)
catsear (common, smooth),
nipplewort, lettuce (wall, prickly)
mouse-ear hawkweed
fox-and-cubs, hawkweed
oxtongue (bristly, hawkweed)
hawksbeards
(smooth, rough, marsh, beaked)

Ragwort type which have central disc florets, usually surrounded by an outer ring of ray florets (these may be very small or absent):

ragwort (common, Oxford, hoary, marsh)
groundsel (common, heath, sticky)
elecampane, corn marigold
leopardsbane, goldenrod
coastal gum plant, tansy
pineappleweed, fleabane
ploughman's spikenard
coltsfoot

Dandelion type - all ray florets, no central disc:

SMOOTH SOWTHISTLE
Sonchus oleraceus

Common on rough ground, verges, pathsides, fields, gardens. Stout, branched, hairless, annual 20-150cm. **Flowerheads** Jun-Oct, pale yellow 20-25mm; **leaves** greyish green, lobed with open pointed lobes round the stem.

PERENNIAL OR CORN
SOWTHISTLE *Sonchus arvensis*

Robust perennial 60-200cm tall, widespread on verges, arable land, sea cliffs. **Flowerhead** Jul-Oct, deep yellow up to 5cm; looks raggy; bracts and stalks covered with orange, glandular hairs; **leaves** long with pointed lobes, softly spine-edged, shiny green.

PRICKLY SOWTHISTLE
Sonchus asper

Common in rough grassland, scrub, on waysides. Over-wintering robust, thistle-like perennial. **Flowerheads** Jun-Oct, golden yellow 20-25mm; **leaves** dark shiny green, crisped with spiny edges, clasp the stem with rounded lobes.

DANDELION *Taraxacum sp*
Familiar low perennial with deep taproot; abundant in short grassland; hollow, single-flowered, leafless stems to 25cm contain milky latex. **Flowerheads** Mar-Oct 20-60mm, bracts green, erect and spreading; **leaves** in ground rosette, thin, arrow-shaped side lobes, large triangular end lobe; seeds wind-dispersed on downy parachutes from fruiting 'clock'.

Hawkbits have leaves in a ground rosette, leafless flowering stems up to 40cm often curved; yellow flowers. Common in grassy places, scrub.

ROUGH HAWKBIT *Leontodon hispidus*
Flowerheads Jun-Oct, 25-40mm; grey, red or yellow beneath; bracts unequal.
Drooping buds.

Foliage hairy. Prefers dry, non-acidic soils. Hairy stems and leaves; stem not branched.

LESSER HAWKBIT *Leontodon saxatilis*
Flowerheads Jun-Oct, c.20mm; grey beneath; green bracts equal, almost hairless.

Stem not branched; bristly below, hairless at the top.

AUTUMN HAWKBIT *Leontodon autumnalis*
Flowerheads Jul-Oct, 12-35mm, reddish beneath; **leaves** thin, shiny, lobes sharply pointed.

Stems up to 60cm, branched, almost hairless with a few small scales near the top; bracts taper into the stem.
(see catsear)

MOUSE-EAR HAWKWEED *Pilosella officinarum*
Flowerheads May-Aug, 20mm, pale yellow, red beneath; **leaves** oval, dull green, softly hairy above, white felted below.

Common on dry heath, in quarries, stony banks. Low hairy, carpeting perennial; long rooting runners give rise to dense ground cover.

HAWKWEED *Hieracium agg*

A group of variable perennials up to 1m tall with leafy, branched stems; frequent on rocky grassland, dry banks, quarries, verges; often in large groups.

Flowerheads May-Sep, 20-35mm, yellow; several rows of unequal green bracts beneath florets; **leaves** may be toothed but never lobed, on stems, often also basal.

FOX-AND-CUBS *Pilosella aurantiaca*

Garden escape, naturalised occasionally on road and rail sides, and in rough grassy ground. Long rooting runners create large stands of erect, black-hairy, flowering stems 30-40cm.

Flowerheads Jun-Sep, deep orange, c.15mm, in terminal clusters; **leaves** oval, mostly in ground rosette.

BRISTLY OXTONGUE *Picris echioides*

Rare, bristly biennial on lime-rich stony soils, mainly coastal. Rough, hairy, furrowed stems 30-90cm. **Flowerheads** Jun-Nov, 20-25mm, large outer bracts leaf-like; **leaves** and bracts have bristles rising from prominent white swellings.

HAWKWEED OXTONGUE *Picris hieracioides*

Infrequent in limestone grassland; bristly, furrowed, branched stem 15-70cm, reddish. **Flowerheads** Jul-Oct, 20-30mm; bristly green bracts, outer row spreading; **leaves** rough, wavy-edged, lanceolate.

NIPPLEWORT *Lapsana communis*

Common in a range of habitats – woods, grassland, waste. Leafy widely-branched annual or perennial, up to 2m.

Flowerheads Jul-Sep, c.15mm.; only 8-15 florets, all rayed; bracts form narrow cup; **leaves** hairy, varied, upper pointed, long oval, slightly toothed; lower leaves have large end-lobe and a few small side-lobes.

GOAT'S-BEARD *Tragopogon pratensis*

Erect biennial, frequent in tall grassland. Often overlooked, as flowers resemble grasses when closed in dull weather and late in the day; **leaves** also grass-like; stems 30-100cm contain milky latex.

Flowerheads May-Aug, to 50mm across; florets all rayed, shorter than surrounding prominent, long pointed bracts; seeds wind-dispersed on downy parachutes from large, fruiting 'clock'.

WALL LETTUCE *Mycelis muralis*

Occasional on shady walls, rocky banks. Hairless, branched perennial; thin stems 25-100cm contain milky latex.

Flowerheads Jun-Sep, up to 10mm wide; numerous on short slender, widely-forked branches; only 5 florets, all rayed; bracts form small tube; **leaves** green, bronze or purple, thin, segmented with large end-lobe, wintergreen.

PRICKLY LETTUCE *Lactuca serriola*

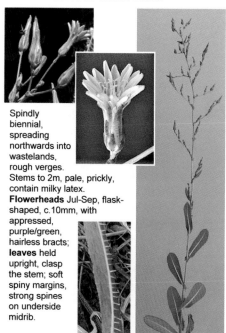

Spindly biennial, spreading northwards into wastelands, rough verges. Stems to 2m, pale, prickly, contain milky latex. **Flowerheads** Jul-Sep, flask-shaped, c.10mm, with appressed, purple/green, hairless bracts; **leaves** held upright, clasp the stem; soft spiny margins, strong spines on underside midrib.

Hawk's-beards are erect branched plants; sepal-like bracts beneath flowerheads are in a single upright inner row surrounded by outer spreading much shorter bracts.

SMOOTH HAWK'S-BEARD *Crepis capillaris*
Widely-branched annual/biennial to 75cm, frequent in open grassy or bare ground. **Flowerheads** Jun-Sep, numerous, 10-13mm across on slender stalks; **leaves** shiny, toothed, mostly in ground rosette; stem leaves clasp with pointed end-lobes.

MARSH HAWK'S-BEARD *Crepis paludosa*
Northern upland, mostly hairless, perennial to 80cm tall, infrequent in wet woodlands, streamsides. **Flowerheads** Jun-Sep, yellow/orange, 15-25mm; **leaves** large, pointed, shiny, arrow-shaped and shallow toothed, clasp the stem with forward-pointing lobes.

ROUGH HAWK'S-BEARD *Crepis biennis*
Stout hairy biennial over 1m tall, local on rough grass-land, verges. **Flowerheads** Jun-Jul, 20-35mm, inner bracts even, unequal outer bracts spreading; **leaves** lobed at base, half clasping on stem; fruits not beaked.

BEAKED HAWK'S-BEARD *Crepis vesicaria*
Mediterranean species moving northwards, locally rare in warm sandy fields. Reddish stems to 80cm. **Flowerheads** May-Jul, 15-25mm, orange beneath; **leaves** downy, basal sharply lobed; fruits long-beaked.

CAT'S-EAR *Hypochaeris radicata*

SMOOTH CAT'S-EAR *Hypochaeris glabra*

Common perennial in grassy, free-draining ground. Stems 20-40cm, often curved, may be branched, with a few small appressed scales.

Flowerheads Jun-Sep, 20-40mm, greyish below; squarish receptacle narrowed abruptly into the stem; unequal green bracts purple-tipped; **leaves** oblong, rough hairy, wavy-edged, all from ground rosette.

Unusual annual of Norfolk Brecklands, very rare in North East Yorkshire. Grows on sandy fields near *Ganton*. **Flowerheads** Jun-Oct, c.10mm, solitary on sprawling stems, only open in full sun; **leaves** narrow, shiny green, slightly lobed.

Ragwort type – centre disc florets, usually with outer ring of ray florets:-

ELECAMPANE *Inula helenium*
Uncommon garden escape; stout leafy perennial to 2.5m tall. **Flowerheads** Jul-Aug, large 6-10cm, narrow ray florets; **leaves** large pointed oval.

COASTAL GUMPLANT *Grindelia stricta*

The only known site in UK for this introduction is on rocky cliffs near *Whitby* harbour, where it grows in low groups amongst native wild cabbage. **Flowerheads** 30-50mm, Jun-Aug; **leaves** finely toothed, stalkless, clasp the stem.

COMMON RAGWORT *Senecio jacobaea*

Common in wasteland or neglected pastures. Erect, branched biennial 30-100cm. **Flowerheads** Jun-Oct, 15-25mm, bracts short, green outer, black-tipped inner; **leaves** unevenly lobed, end-lobe blunt.

OXFORD RAGWORT *Senecio squalidus*

Frequent on well-drained soils, railsides, waste ground. Bushy annual/perennial to 50cm. **Flowerheads** Apr-Nov, 16-20mm across; all bracts tipped black; **leaf** lobes narrow, pointed.

MARSH RAGWORT *Senecio aquaticus*

Occasional biennial in wet grassland, ponds, ditches, marshes; stems to 80cm. **Flowerheads** Jul-Aug, 25-30mm across, flat; disc and ray florets yellow; **leaves** shiny with large oval, often toothed, end-lobe and a few small or no side-lobes.

HOARY RAGWORT *Senecio erucifolius*

Biennial up to 1m tall, appears greyish with fine hairs on stem and leaves. **Flowerheads** Jul-Sep, 15-20mm, pale yellow; bracts pale green; **leaf** lobes narrow, pointed, with incurved margins. Uncommon inland, frequent along the coast.

PINEAPPLEWEED *Matricaria discoidea*

Common on fertile ground in gateways, fields, tracks. Much-branched short annual, smells of pineapple. **Flowerheads** May-Nov, cone 5-8mm of green/yellow disc florets in cup of green, pale-edged bracts; normally no ray florets; **leaves** finely divided into hair-like segments.

COMMON GROUNDSEL *Senecio vulgaris*
Short annual to c.30cm, common on open and disturbed ground. **Flowerheads** Jan-Dec, only 4mm across, packed in a tube of bracts, short outer row black-tipped, long inner row mainly green; ray florets unusual; **leaves** narrow, blunt-lobed.

Unusual rayed form

HEATH GROUNDSEL *Senecio sylvaticus*

Scattered in open habitats, felled plantations, coastal cliffs. Faintly aromatic, slightly glandular annual 30-70cm tall. **Flowerheads** Jul-Sep, 5mm, with short, recurved ray florets; long inner bracts black tipped; outer bracts tiny; **leaves** long narrow, cottony lobes.

STICKY GROUNDSEL *Senecio viscosus*

Strong-smelling annual, occasional in well-drained habitats, often coastal. Glandular hairy stems to 60cm. **Flowerheads** Jul-Sep, 8mm; long inner bracts rarely dark-tipped, outer bracts all green, half the length of inner bracts; **leaves** dark green, covered with sticky glandular hairs.

CORN MARIGOLD *Chrysanthemum segetum*

LEOPARD'S-BANE *Doronicum pardalianches*

Also known as 'golds'; once abundant, now rare in arable land. Hairless, greyish annual, 20-50cm stems. **Flowerheads** Jun-Oct, solitary, up to 50mm across; blunt ray florets bright yellow, centre disc florets darker; **leaves** smooth, narrow oval with shallow lobes.

Tall perennial, introduced as a medicinal plant, naturalised occasionally in woods, on verges. Stems to 1m tall, hairy. **Flowerheads** Apr-Jul, 4-6cm, bright yellow; **leaves** large cordate, clasping on stems, long-stalked from the ground.

COMMON FLEABANE *Pulicaria dysenterica*

COLT'S-FOOT *Tussilago farfara*

Sometimes numerous in ditches and damp waysides, abundant on sea-cliff seepages. Creeping, patch-forming perennial has hairy, branched stems, upright to 1m. **Flowerheads** Aug-Sep, up to 30mm across, golden yellow disc, paler ray florets; **leaves** oblong, wavy-edged, very downy, clasp upper stems.

Short pioneer plant, widespread on bare tracks, spoil heaps, rough grassy ground; frequent on slumped coastal cliffs. Spreading, early-flowering perennial; thick, scaly stems 5-15cm tall with solitary flowers. **Flowerheads** Mar-Apr, c.30mm, bracts narrow, purplish, beneath yellow florets; **leaves** long-stalked, appear later, roundish, shallow-lobed, white felted beneath.

GOLDENROD
Solidago virgaurea
Infrequent perennial on rocky banks, streamside, sea cliffs. Leafy stems 5-70cm tall. **Flowerheads** Jun-Sep, 6-10mm, have few, short yellow ray florets, orange/yellow centre disc florets; **leaves** dark green, oval, hairless.

CANADIAN GOLDENROD *Solidago canadensis*
Much larger than native goldenrod, a frequent garden escape, grows over 2m tall; tiny **flowerheads** Jul-Sep, on long side branches; **leaves** softly hairy, narrow, pointed.

PLOUGHMAN'S SPIKENARD *Inula conyzae*

Uncommon on dry, lime-rich stony ground. Downy stems, erect to 1m, often reddish. **Flowerheads** Jul-Sep, up to 10mm across, in large sprays; deep yellow upright disc florets, occasionally a few tiny ray florets; bracts green, tipped red/brown, in unequal rows, lower ones spreading or recurved.

Leaves deeply veined, large pointed oval; ground rosette ± evergreen.

TANSY *Tanacetum vulgare*

Grows occasionally on grassy road and river sides, sea cliffs. Strong-smelling, hairless perennial, erect to 1m. **Flowerheads** Jul-Oct, button-like, only 1cm across, many in flat, stem-top spray; deep yellow disc florets, usually no ray florets, on small flat receptacle with short green bracts; **leaves** dark green, deeply divided into evenly-toothed leaflets.

ORCHID FAMILY *ORCHIDACEAE*

Perennials with erect stems topped with a flowering spike; simple, untoothed, parallel-veined leaves; flowers have 3 outer and 3 inner segments, usually all similar colour; often lowest inner segment forms a lip (labellum); many orchids attract pollinating insects by nectar secreted in a spur; single stamen has two pollen masses (pollinia); flowering spikes appear erratically.

COMMON SPOTTED ORCHID *Dactylorhiza fuchsii*

Common, often numerous, in varied non-acidic habitats, verges, scrub, meadow, marshes. Solid stem 15-40cm; **flowers** Jun-Aug, light pink with darker marks; upper hood, 2 spreading side segments, labellum with <u>middle lobe equal to or longer than side lobes</u>, conical spur; **leaves** grey/green with transverse dark blotches.

HEATH SPOTTED ORCHID *Dactylorhiza maculata*

Scattered in more acidic soils, heaths, moors. Stem solid 15-40cm; **flowers** Jun-Aug, very pale pink with darker marks; upper hood, 2 spreading side segments, labellum with <u>tiny pointed middle lobe</u> not extending beyond frilly side lobes, conical spur; **leaves** narrow, pointed.

EARLY MARSH ORCHID *Dactylorhiza incarnata*

Scarce in marsh, damp meadow. Hollow stem 20-60cm. **Flowers** May-Jul, light reddish pink with darker marks; upper hood, side segments almost erect; labellum folded backwards to appear narrow, has 3 small lobes; straight tapering spur; long green bracts extend above flowers; **leaves** unspotted, yellow/green, keeled and narrowing to hooded tip.

NORTHERN MARSH ORCHID *Dactylorhiza purpurella*

Northern plant, occasional in non-acidic grassy places, marsh, verges, coastal cliffs. Stubby 10-25cm stem (hybrids taller). **Flowers** Jun-Jul, deep purple with dark marks; upper hood and spreading side segments; labellum diamond-shaped, unlobed; stout spur; **leaves** short, broad, usually dark-spotted at the tip.

ORCHIDS 167

NARROW-LEAVED MARSH ORCHID
Dactylorhiza traunsteineri
Slender, very infrequent orchid grows in small numbers in calcareous wetland. **Flowers** May-Jun, fewer than 12 on 20-40cm flexuous stem; lilac to deep purple, darker markings on the labellum which has large central lobe; stout spur points down; **leaves** narrow, keeled, may have tiny spots near the tip.

FRAGRANT ORCHID
Gymnadenia conopsea
Elegant fragrant plant, occasional in base-rich fen and limestone grassland. Stem to 40cm. **Flowers** Jun-Jul, rose pink, few or no markings; upper hood, 2 side segments spreading, narrow, pointed; labellum wide 3-lobed; curved slender spur up to 20mm long; **leaves** glossy green, unspotted, strongly keeled.

BEE ORCHID *Ophrys apifera*
Scattered in small numbers on lime-rich banks, quarries, sea-cliffs, grassy scrub. Attracts insect pollinators by resembling a bee with a 'furry' lower lip.

FLY ORCHID *Ophrys insectifera*
Appears erratically, sometimes in large numbers, on lime-rich turf or scree; attracts insect pollinators by its fly-like structure.

Stem 10-40cm. **Flowers** Jun-Jul, 3 large pink outer segments surround small green hooded segment, 2 part-erect green side segments and large lower lip, 'furry' brown with coloured markings; **leaves** green.

Stem 10- 40cm. **Flowers** May-Jun, short-stalked, wide-spaced up the stem; 3 green outer segments; other segments are coloured and arranged to resemble a fly; **leaves** shiny, floppy lower down, upper stem leaves few, small.

PYRAMIDAL ORCHID *Anacamptis pyramidalis*

Occasional, on calcareous well-drained soils, verges, sea cliffs, grassy scrub. **Flower** spike Jun-Aug, cone-shaped on stem 20-30cm; flowers deep pink, scarcely marked, hooded and 2 spreading outer segments; labellum broad with 3 divergent equal lobes; spur very slender, straight.

Leaves unspotted, green.

EARLY PURPLE ORCHID *Orchis mascula*

Away from acidic soils, frequent in woods, hedgebanks; strong smelling late in the day. Stem solid, fleshy 20-40cm; **leaves** shiny, dark green with elongated dark blotches.

Flowers Apr-Jun, bright purple (rarely white), hooded, 2 spreading side segments; labellum 3-lobed, broad with sides folded back, pale in centre, spur curves upwards.

GREEN-WINGED ORCHID *Orchis morio*

Formerly a common grassland orchid but susceptible to herbicides, now very rare. **Flowers** Apr-Jun, fragrant, at top of 10-30cm stem; hood and 2 upright side wings pink/purple with dark green stripes; lip purple/white, broad, folded back, lobed front edge.

Leaves glossy green, unspotted.
Hole of Horcum

BURNT ORCHID *Orchis ustulata*

Rare, mainly southern orchid of unimproved calcareous grassland, has one known local site in a sheltered valley near *Newton-on-Rawcliffe*. Stem only 5-15cm with short dense spike; buds dark purple, open to white **flowers** May-Jun; lobed lower lip dotted red; small black/purple hood and tiny spur; **leaves** oval, mostly in basal rosette.

BROAD-LEAVED HELLEBORINE
Epipactis helleborine

Infrequent in open woodland and shady hedgebanks; spreads by runners. One-sided flowering spike up to 60cm tall. **Flowers** Jul-Sep, greenish mauve, hooded; 2 purple striated spreading side segments; centre segment cup-shaped with roundish pink lip, no spur; **leaves** broad oval, deeply veined.

MARSH HELLEBORINE
Epipactis palustris

Rare in calcareous marshes where it spreads by runners. Stem 15-50cm, part downy; **Flowers** Jul-Aug, have 3 green/ purple outer segments; lower inner segments have reddish centre cup with frilly-edged white lip; **leaves** pleated, strongly veined, half clasping the stem.

GREATER BUTTERFLY ORCHID
Platanthera chlorantha
Infrequent in small numbers on calcareous pasture or in woodland. Erect hairless stem 30-60cm. **Leaves** 2 broad, oval at the base; a few small stem leaves.

LESSER BUTTERFLY ORCHID
Platanthera bifolia
Smaller than greater butterfly orchid; stem 15-30 cm. **Flowers** May-Jul, have pollinia which lie parallel and close together; long almost straight spur; the two shining basal **leaves** tend to be broader and shorter.
Tolerates more acidic ground; very infrequent on moorland or in woods.

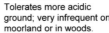

Flowers Jun-Jul, fragrant, green/ cream; short hood over 2 diverging pollinia, 2 spreading side-segments; narrow pointed lip hangs down; spur up to 30mm long, curved.

FROG ORCHID *Coeloglossum viride*

Formerly quite common in calcareous short pasture, quarries, scrub. Much decreased after grassland 'improvement'. Emergence of flowering spikes erratic from year to year. Erect stem 4-20cm.

Flowers Jun-Aug; hood and 2 side segments curve inwards; long hanging lip with short central lobe and 2 longer side lobes; short blunt spur; **leaves** basal and on stem.

© ALAN RITSON

SMALL WHITE ORCHID *Pseudorchis albida*

An upland plant frequent in Scotland, growing on mountain pastures and cliff ledges; scarce elsewhere in UK, its only known local site is on *Fylingdales Moor* where it flowers intermittently. Erect stem to 30cm.

Flowers in a dense spike May-Jun; fragrant, greenish white; lower lip deeply cut into 3 lobes; short spur; **leaves** broad basal and narrow up the stem.

© ALAN RITSON

COMMON TWAYBLADE *Listera ovata*

Occasional in woods and grassy verges. Sturdy all-green orchid, erect stem 20-60cm. **Flowers** Jun-Jul, green, without markings; upper segments curve in to form hood; lower lip deeply forked, hangs down; no spur;

leaves stalkless, 2 large, oval, ribbed blades a short way up the stem.

LESSER TWAYBLADE *Listera cordata*
Rare in acidic damp woods and moorland. Like a tiny common twayblade, under 10cm stem; 2 shiny green roundish leaves; **flowers** buff/pink, deeply-lobed lip.

BIRD'S-NEST ORCHID *Neottia nidus-avis*

Locally very rare in beech or mixed woods. A saprophytic herb lacking green colouring; buff erect stem 20-40cm. **Flowers** May-Jul, have hood and long 2-lobed lip but no spur; **leaves** absent; brownish scales on the stem.

LILY FAMILY LILIACEAE

Mostly bulbous plants with long narrow leaves; flowers with 3 petals and 3 sepals (often of the same colour to appear as 6 petals – all referred to here as petals).

SNOWDROP *Galanthus nivalis*

C16th introduction, widely naturalised especially near habitation. Spreads by division of its small bulb. **Flowers** Jan-Mar, single on 10-25cm stalks; 3 white outer segments, 3 shorter, notched inner petals, with green marks, form hanging bell; **leaves** 4mm wide grey/green.

PLEATED SNOWDROP *Galanthus plicatus*

Garden introduction from Turkey, occasionally naturalised in woods and damp grassland. Differs from common snowdrop by its wide, green **leaves**, glaucous on top, stronger mid vein and edges folded back; also larger green marks on inner petals.

SUMMER SNOWFLAKE *Leucojum aestivum*

Garden introduction, infrequently naturalised in light shade. Up to 60cm tall stems have several **flowers** Apr-May; all 6 petals alike with green mark and upturned end; **leaves** lax, broad and bright green.

STAR-OF-BETHLEHEM *Ornithogalum angustifolium*

Garden introduction, infrequently naturalised on verge or wasteland. Starry **flowers** May-Jun, c.3cm across, green striped on back; **leaves** linear with pale central stripe.

YELLOW STAR-OF-BETHLEHEM *Gagea lutea*

Short bulbous perennial, rare in lime-rich damp woodland, shady riverside. **Flowers** Feb-May, 20mm, 6 petals yellow above, green below;

leaves linear with hooded blunt tip and 3 prominent veins beneath the blade.

BLUEBELL *Hyacinthoides non-scripta*

Bulbous perennial, carpets woods and shady banks. Up to 12 blue (rarely white) bells, with 6 recurved tips and cream anthers, hang on one side of drooping spike 20-50cm tall

Apr-May; **leaves** linear, hairless, shiny green, all basal.

SPANISH BLUEBELL *Hyacinthoides sp*

Both Spanish and hybrids with native bluebell are garden plants often established in the wild. Can be blue, pink, mauve, white. Bells hang all round more erect

spikes; bell tips less recurved; anthers dark.

LILY-OF-THE-VALLEY *Convallaria majalis*

Fragrant patch-forming perennial, rare in ash woods. **Flowers** May-Jun, 6-lobed small bells on side of slender, hairless stem 10-20cm tall; **leaves** parallel-veined, grow from the ground in pairs. **Fruit** a red berry.

BOG ASPHODEL *Narthecium ossifragum*

Creeping, hairless perennial, often extensive in wet acidic heath or flush. **Flowers** Jul-Aug, bright yellow stars c.15mm across with 6 orange anthers; fading petals orange; stems upright 10-40cm; **leaves** flat linear, curve upwards from the ground.

HERB-PARIS *Paris quadrifolia*
Low colonial all-green perennial, difficult to see in a carpet of dog's mercury. Infrequent in damp ancient woodland on limestone. Hairless erect stems 15-40cm.

Flowers May-Jul, solitary in a flat whorl of 4 pointed, narrow, green sepals and 4 (3,6 or 7) narrow green petals around 8 upright stamens and a purple round ovary; later forms a berry; **leaves** net-veined, large pointed oval, usually 4, in a flat whorl below the flower.

WILD DAFFODIL *Narcissus pseudonarcissus*

Bulbous perennial, native in old ash and oak woods and on river banks. Shorter and paler than alien varieties planted on verges and amenity ground. Spreads extensively in light damp shade. **Flowers** Mar-Apr, solitary on flattened stalk; outer whorl of 6 pale petals surround deeper yellow narrow trumpet c.30mm long; **leaves** flat linear, grey/green.

MAY LILY *Maianthemum bifolium*   Nationally rare, creeping perennial on free-draining acidic soil has two small populations near *Forge Valley*. Extensive carpet of cordate, deep-veined **leaves** on 8-20cm stalks. **Flowers** May-Jun, 4-lobed on short stalks, but flowering spikes very rare in local plants.

SOLOMON'S SEAL *Polygonatum multiflorum*
Rare in ash woodland on limestone. Leafy perennial with arching stems, grows in small clumps in light shade.

Flowers May-Jun, white bells, narrowed midway, with 6 incurved green tips; **leaves** all on stems, broad oval, parallel-veined; **fruit** blue/black berries.

Beadale, Ashberry, Newtondale.

BUTCHER'S BROOM *Ruscus aculeatus*
Evergreen introduced dioecious small shrub, rare in dry woodland. Tiny, pale green 6-petalled **flowers** Jan-Apr, grow on sharply-pointed, oval, leaf-like stems; **fruit** a red berry late in autumn but not known to develop on local plants.
Glaisdale, Forge Valley.

MEADOW SAFFRON
Colchicum autumnale
Colourful, crocus-like, late-flowering corm, introduced and naturalised in a fieldside near *Byland Abbey*.
Flowers Aug-Oct without **leaves** which emerge in spring. Differs from crocus by its 6 stamens (crocus 3).

RAMSONS or WILD GARLIC *Allium ursinum*

Dense carpeter with strong garlic smell, widespread in nutrient-rich soils in damp woods. Stems to 45cm. **Flowers** Apr-Jun, starry 5-petalled; **leaves** long-stalked, large, strap-like, pointed.

SAND LEEK *Allium scorodoprasum*
Infrequent in dry, rough grassy places; purple **flowers** May-Aug, c.5mm long, grow from globe of purple bulbils; 2 short papery bracts beneath flowerhead; **leaves** grass-like, flat, keeled, rough-edged.

FEW-FLOWERED GARLIC
Allium paradoxum
Scarce in woods, waste; numerous green bulbils but only 1 or 2 white bell **flowers** Apr-May, 10-12mm long; 2 short white bracts; a single **leaf**, narrow, strongly keeled.

FIELD GARLIC
Allium oleraceum
Rare on dry grassland; green/mauve bulbils; **flowers** Jul-Aug, 6-7mm on long thin stalks; 2 very long papery bracts; **leaves** channelled.

FLOWERING-RUSH FAMILY BUTOMACEAE

FLOWERING-RUSH *Butomus umbellatus*

Showy, lowland, water-edge plant to 1.5m tall. Rare in lime-rich *Costa Beck*. **Flowers** Jul-Sep, soft pink, cup-shaped, stalked in open umbel; **leaves** long, twisted ± triangular.

IRIS FAMILY IRIDACEAE

YELLOW FLAG IRIS
Iris pseudacorus
Showy perennial up to 1.5m
tall,often forms large stands in
fresh water, marshes. **Flowers**
Jun-Aug, 8-10 cm across, have
3 dark striated outer petals, 3
curved inner petals, 3 petal-like
stamens and yellow styles;
leaves stout sword-shaped.

MONTBRETIA
Crocosmia x crocosmiiflora
Widely naturalised garden escape,
especially on coastal cliffs. Waving
stems to 1m tall cover extensive
patches. **Flowers** Jul-Oct, bright
orange, 6 petalled, funnel shaped,
grow on one side of long flattened
spike; **leaves** sword-like with raised
midrib.

ARUM FAMILY ARACEAE

WILD ARUM *Arum maculatum*
LORDS-AND-LADIES

From Feb. onwards, arum's large,
arrow-shaped shiny, green **leaves**,
sometimes with dark blotches,
emerge on hedgebanks and wood
edge with enriched soil; leaves are
followed by a spathe or thin leaf-like
cowl which protects a smelly purple
prong or spadix.

SWEET-FLAG *Acorus calamus*
Infrequent introduction forms a dense
mass of sword-shaped leaves in
shallow lakeside. **Leaves** over 1m,
have crinkled edge, strong off-centre
vein; aromatic when
crushed. **Flowers** Jun-
Jul. Spadix 5-9cm
long, growing from
stem side; shy to
flower.

The spadix
attracts insects
which drop into
the enclosed
lower spathe,
thereby pollinating
tiny hidden
flowers, Mar-Apr.
Poisonous red
berries mature on
spikes 30-50cm
tall, Jul-Aug.

WATER-PLANTAIN FAMILY ALISMATACEAE

WATER-PLANTAIN *Alisma plantago-aquatica*
Waterside, widely-
branched perennial
up to 1m tall,
occasional in ditches,
streams and ponds.

LESSER WATER-PLANTAIN
Baldelia ranunculoides
Low or creeping perennial, rare in ditch or
stream with shallow, peaty water away
from stronger competing vegetation.
Flowers Jun-Aug, mauve/white up to
15mm, long-stalked; **leaves** stalked,
narrow, pointed blades; fragrant when
crushed.

Flowers Jun-Aug, 10mm across,
open after midday with 3 green
sepals, 3 pinkish/white petals
and 6 stamens; fruits arranged in
a flattened circular disc; **leaf**
blades large pointed oval on long
stalks.

WATER-STARWORT FAMILY CALLITRICHACEAE

WATER-STARWORT
Callitriche spp
Small aquatic herbs,
frequent in muddy pools
and shallow water.
Small opposite **leaves**
congested to from a star
on water surface;
flowers tiny, obscure.

FROGBIT FAMILY HYDROCHARITACEAE

WATERWEED *Elodea spp*
Introduced as pond or fish-
tank oxygenators, often
naturalised in fresh water.
Submerged dark green,
translucent, curled leaves
form thick mass. Propagates
vegetatively; only female
plants in UK; flowers obscure.

WATER LILY FAMILY NYMPHAEACEAE

YELLOW WATER-LILY *Nuphar lutea*
Uncommon due to shortage of still or slow-moving
water. Occasionally planted.
Flowers Jul-Aug, 4-6cm, rich
yellow, bowl-shaped, enclosing
many large yellow stamens;
flowers single on stems which
project above water level;
leaves cordate oval, floating;
fruit roundish with narrow
neck topped by flat disc.

WHITE WATER-LILY *Nymphaea alba*
Forms large floating rafts of
flowers and leaves on open or
slow-moving water, usually in
man-made habitat. **Flowers**
Jun-Sep, 10-20cm, with more
than 20 inward-curved white
petals, yellow stamens;
leaves cordate round, floating;
fruit almost round.

MARE'S-TAIL FAMILY HIPPURIDACEAE

MARE'S-TAIL
Hippuris vulgaris
Uncommon in slow lime-
rich stream or pond.
Underwater stems
produce upright shoots to
1m with whorls of strap-
shaped leaves. **Flowers**
Jun-Jul, tiny greenish, in
leaf axils.

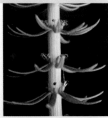

WATER-MILFOIL FAMILY HALORGRACEAE

WATER-MILFOIL
Myriophyllum sp
Infrequent aquatic herbs in
lakes and slow-moving water.
Submerged foliage has whorls
divided into fine linear
segments. Emergent flowering
spikes with tiny flowers in bract
axils, Jun-Aug.

BUR-REED FAMILY SPARGANIACEAE

BRANCHED BUR-REED *Sparganium erectum*
Frequent water's edge perennial away from grazing
cattle. Stout branched stems to 1.5m tall. **Flowers**
Jun-Aug, in balls, small male at top, large female
lower down; **fruits** form in spiky round heads; **leaves**
keeled.

UNBRANCHED BUR-REED *Sparganium emersum*
is smaller, has some floating leaves and prefers
deeper water; not common.

BULRUSH FAMILY TYPHACEAE

BULRUSH or REEDMACE
Typha latifolia
Robust 3m tall colonial perennial,
occasional in shallow water or
marsh. Tiny female **flowers** Jun-
Aug, packed into brown sausage-
shaped spike, immediately below a
thinner fawn male spike (space
separates m and f spikes in locally
very rare **lesser bulrush**); seeds
blow away as fluffy down; **leaves**
long, greyish, slightly twisted.

ARROWGRASS FAMILY *JUNCAGINACEAE*

Wetland perennials with long, narrow, fleshy basal leaves and erect flowering stems to 60cm tall;

MARSH ARROWGRASS
Triglochin palustre is frequent in coastal and inland marshes. Purple-tinted **flowers** Jun-Aug, <u>spaced</u> on spike; **fruits** appear arrow-shaped when valves split to release seeds; **leaves** deeply furrowed.

SEA ARROWGRASS
Triglochin maritimum occurs in saltmarsh at *Whitby* and *Ruswarp*, also in sea-cliff wetland. Green **flowers** May-Aug, densely <u>packed</u> on spikes; **fruits** globular, soon fall off; **leaves** not furrowed.

DUCKWEED FAMILY *LEMNACEAE*

COMMON DUCKWEED
Lemna minor
Very common floating annual in still or sluggish water. Fronds rounded c.8mm.

IVY-LEAVED DUCKWEED *L. trisulca*
Uncommon in still or brackish water. Fronds 7-12mm translucent, oval, float just below the water surface. Divided fronds lie at right angles.

LEAST DUCKWEED
Lemna minuta
Recent introduction; floating fronds tiny oval, 0.5-2.5 mm.

PONDWEED FAMILY *POTAMOGETONACEAE*

Freshwater aquatic perennials with floating or submerged leaves; small flowers on short erect spikes.

Broad-leaved Pondweed *Potamogeton.natans* is widespread in shallow still or slow-moving water. Green or bronze, broad oval, floating leaf blades have parallel convergent <u>pale veins</u> and buff ring at joint with long submerged stems; dense flower spikes erect to 8cm May-Sep. **Bog Pondweed** *P.polygonifolius* is similar but leaf blades are <u>dark veined</u> and show no joint with the stem; restricted to acid water. Also recorded in the area are **Red Pondweed** *P. alpinus,* **Lesser Pondweed** *P.pusillus,* **Curled Pondweed** *P.crispus,* **Various-leaved Pondweed** *P.gramineus* and **Opposite-leaved Pondweed** *Groenlandia densa.*

GLOSSARY

achene	small, dry fruit, shed before releasing the seed.
alien	plant believed to have been introduced by man and now naturalised.
annual	plant which completes its life cycle from seed to fruit in one year.
anther	pollen sac on a stalk (filament) which together form a stamen or male part of a flower.
apical	tip furthest away from point of attachment.
appressed	lying flat, usually refers to hairs close to stem or leaf.
awn	bristle or hair-like projection, e.g. at a leaf or sepal end.
base-rich (basic)	soil or water rich in alkaline nutrients.
beak	terminal projection on a fruit.
berry	fleshy fruit containing seeds eg. gooseberry.
bifid	split into two parts.
blade	part of a leaf beyond the stalk; shape assists species identification.
bract	modified leaf:
	1. beneath flower petals where it may be green leaf-like or petal-colour.
	2. tiny growth on some stems e.g. catsear.
	3. sepal-like leaf at base of main (lower) umbel.
bracteole	on umbels, small leaves at base of secondary (upper) umbel.
bulbil	small bulb produced on a flowerhead or in a leaf axil.
caesious	blue/grey colour.
calcicole	plant which will not grow on acid soil.
calcifuge	plant which will not grow on limy soil.
calyx	outer whorl of a flower enclosing petals in bud; usually green but may be petal-coloured in some species replacing petals; a calyx consists of sepals which may be fused into a tube, or separate leaf or bract-like.
capsule	dry fruit from which seeds are released through holes or splits.
casual	alien plant which appears occasionally but not regularly.
chlorophyll	green colouring which enables flowering plants (except saprophytes) to create growth-essential carbohydrates.
cordate	heart-shaped e.g. oval or round leaf with 2 rounded basal lobes.
corm	underground stem enlarged to store plant nutrients, usually replaced annually.
crenate	edged with rounded teeth.
dioecious	species with male and female flowers on separate plants.
disc	in daisy type plants, the centre mass of florets without rays or 'petals'.
eutrophic	rich in plant nutrients.
florets	tiny flowers usually tightly packed into a composite flowerhead e.g. daisy.
flush	wet area on moorland caused by water spreading laterally above ground.
glabrous	without hairs.
gland	coloured or translucent pore or swelling secreting oil, water or sugar.
glaucous	bluish colour.
habitat	area with similar features relative to plant requirements, therefore likely to be inhabited by a particular range of plants.
hood	upper petal, usually curved.
keel	two petals or leaf folded in V formation resembling a boat keel.
labellum	lowest petal adapted by shape or colouring to attract pollinating insects to a flower.
latex	watery or milky or coloured fluid contained in some species, shows in a broken stem or leaf.
leaflet	small leaf-like segment of a divided leaf.
lip	usually larger, and may be cleft, lower petal of plants such as orchids and mints.
native	established species which arrived naturally, not a human introduction.
nectary	a nectar-bearing organ.
node	part of a stem where a leaf or leaves are attached; sometimes swollen.
nut	dry single-seeded hard fruit.

ochrea	in the dock family, tubular often fringed membrane around leaf attachment.
ovary	on a female flower, an oval or round sac containing ovules (unripe seeds) and extended into a pollen tube(s) or style(s).
palmate	describes a leaf with more than 3 leaflets arising together at the stalk top.
parasitic	without green chlorophyll and deriving nutrients by means of suckers on another species; partial parasites have some green leaves.
pedicel	a flower stalk.
perennial	plant which requires two years or more to flower, fruit and seed.
petals	parts of a flower, usually coloured, which surround stamens and ovary.
petiole	a leaf stalk.
pinnate	compound leaf with separate leaflets attached to a leaf stalk.
pollinia	sticky masses of pollen grains attached to orchid anthers, often transferred to other plants by visiting insects.
ray floret	on daisy-type flower, outer florets with petal-like extension.
receptacle	broad top of flower stalk where flower parts (sepals, petals, stamens, ovaries) are attached.
reflexed	bent backwards or downwards.
saprophytic	describes a plant, usually without green colouring, which takes part or all of its food from dying or dead organic matter.

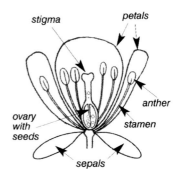

sepal	small leaf-like structure, usually green, lies outside petals (occasionally replacing them).
serrate	edged with saw-like teeth.
sessile	without a stalk.
simple	leaf blade not divided into leaflets.
sp.	single species.
spp.	more than one species.
ssp.	sub-species.
spathe	large bract enclosing a flower e.g. arum.
spur	hollow projection from a petal or sepal, usually containing nectar.
stamen	male flower part comprising filaments (stalk) topped by anthers (sacs containing pollen).
standard	upper or top petal of a pea-type flower or an erect inner segment in an iris-type flower.
stigma	in the female part of a flower, sticky top of a style (stalk) where pollen grains are deposited.
stolon	rooting stem above ground.
style	stalk joining flower ovary to stigma, enabling movement of pollen grains.
tendril	on a climbing or scrambling plant, a modified stem, leaf or stalk which twists around nearby support.
tomentose	covered with dense, short, fine hairs.
trifoliate	leaf with 3 leaflets arising from the same point e.g. clover.
umbel	plant with domed or flat-topped arrangement of small flowers on stalks arising like umbrella spokes from the top of a single stem.
whorl	leaves, bracts or flowers growing in a ring round a stem.
wings	2 side petals on a pea-type flower.

182

APPENDIX A

The Botanical Society of the British Isles receives plant records from botanists throughout the country. In 2002 it published The New Atlas of the British and Irish Flora. The following maps, extracted from the Atlas, illustrate how some upland and lowland species extend into North East Yorkshire, augmenting its floral diversity. Climate change could cause some northern species to migrate northwards, disappearing from this area and being replaced by new warmth-loving southern species moving here.

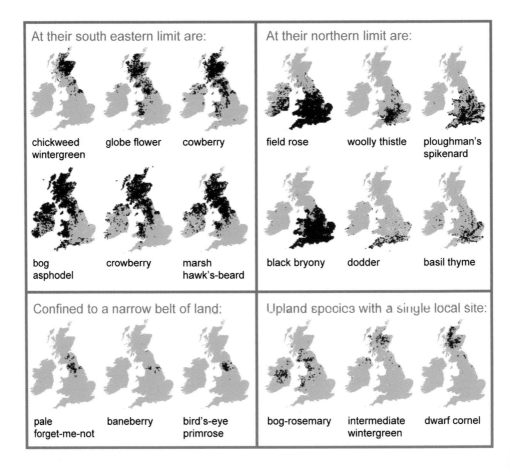

At their south eastern limit are:			At their northern limit are:		
chickweed wintergreen	globe flower	cowberry	field rose	woolly thistle	ploughman's spikenard
bog asphodel	crowberry	marsh hawk's-beard	black bryony	dodder	basil thyme

Confined to a narrow belt of land:			Upland species with a single local site:		
pale forget-me-not	baneberry	bird's-eye primrose	bog-rosemary	intermediate wintergreen	dwarf cornel

APPENDIX B

During the C20th many resident and visiting botanists explored the flora of North East Yorkshire, recording their findings in books and pamphlets, or amassing herbarium specimens now conserved in the Pannett Museum at Whitby and in the Yorkshire Museum at York. They provide locations for records throughout the area as well as detailed lists for the Howardian Hills, Scarborough, Goathland and Whitby. Comparison of today's flora with these records reveals that at least 40 wild flowers have become extinct in this region, largely due to changes in farming practices, drainage and afforestation. Many surviving species are reduced to fragmented populations in only one or two sites and are regarded as on the edge of survival.

Locally extinct:

Great sundew *(drosera anglica)*
Oblong-leaved sundew *(drosera intermedia)*
Maiden pink *((dianthus deltoides)*
Water germander *(teucrium scordium)*
Lesser skullcap *(scutellaria minor)*
Lesser water-parsnip *(sium latifolium)*
Pheasant's-eye *(adonis annua)*
Jacob's ladder *(polemonium caeruleum)*
Wild tulip *(tulipa sylvestris)*
Weasel's-snout *(misopates orontium)*
Narrow-leaved helleborine *(cephalanthera longifolia)*
Nettle-leaved bellflower *(campanula trachelium)*
Marsh gentian *(gentaina pneumonanthe)*
Yellow figwort *(scrophularia vernalis)*
Vervain *(verbena officinalis)*
Round-leaved wintergreen *(pyrola rotundifolia)*
Shepherd's cress *(teesdalia nudicaulis)*
Corncockle *(agrostemma githago)*
Perennial flax *(linum perenne)*
Allseed *(radiola linoides)*
Wild liquorice *(astragalus glycophyllos)*
Sickle medick *(medicago falcata)*
Wormwood *(artemisia absinthium)*
Bur-marigolds *(bidens spp)*
Lady's slipper orchid *(cypripedium calceolus)*
Autumn lady's-tresses *(spiranthes spiralis)*
Marsh stitchwort *(stellaria palustris)*
Sea lavender *(limonium vulgare)*
Cotton thistle *(ornithopodium acanthium)*
Wild parsnip *(pastinaca sativa)*
White horehound *(marrubium vulgare)*
Cowbane *(cicuta virosa)*
Mousetail *(myuros minimus)*
Purple milk-vetch *(astragalus danicus)*
Field gentian *(gentianella campestris)*

Locally decreased, now very rare:

Dwarf thistle *(cirsium acaule)*
Marsh St.John's-wort *(hypericum elodes)*
Pale St. John's-wort *(hypericum montanum)*
Deadly nightshade *(atropa belladonna)*
Henbane *(hyoscyamus niger)*
Greater sea spurrey *(spergularia media)*
Great lettuce *(lactuca virosa)*
Shepherd's needle *(scandix pecten-veneris)*
Prickly poppy *(papaver argemone)*
Greater spearwort *(ranunculus lingua)*
Small-white orchid *(pseudorchis albida)*
Frog orchid *(coeloglossum viride)*
Green-winged orchid *(orchis morio)*
Intermediate wintergreen *(pyrola media)*
Petty spurge *(euphorbia exigua)*
Large hemp-nettle *(galeopsis speciosa)*
Red hemp-nettle *(galeopsis angustifolia)*
Mountain everlasting *(antennaria dioica)*
Marsh cinquefoil *(potentilla palustris)*
Columbine *(aquilegia vulgaris)*
Fine-leaved fumitory *(fumaria parviflora)*
Night-flowering catchfly *(silene noctiflora)*
Venus's looking-glass *(legousia hybrida)*
Narrow-fruited cornsalad *(valerianella dentata)*
Hound's-tongue *(cynoglossum officinale)*
Bird's-eye primrose *(primula farinosa)*
Dyer's greenweed *(genista tinctoria)*
Corn marigold *(chrysanthemum segetum)*
Meadow-rue *(thalictrum flavum)*
Lesser butterfly orchid *(platanthera bifolia)*
Burnt orchid *(orchis ustulata)*
Marsh helleborine *(epipactis palustris)*
Treacle mustard *(erysimum cheiranthoides)*
Lesser water-plantain *(baldelia ranunculoides)*
Sea aster *(aster tripolium)*
Bog-rosemary *(andromeda polifolia)*
Hairy rock-cress *(arabis hirsuta)*
Basil thyme *(clinopodium acinos)*
Wild clary *(salvia verbenaca)*
Cornflower *(centaurea cyanus)*
Water violet *(hottonia palustris)*
Bithynian vetch *(vicia bithynica)*
Corn buttercup *(ranunculus arvensis)*
Lesser marshwort *(apium inundatum)*
Long-stalked crane's-bill
          (geranium columbinum)

184

Suggested further reading:

New Atlas of the British & Irish Flora.
C.D.Preston, D.A.Pearman, T.D.Dines (2002) Oxford University Press

The Wild Flowers of the British Isles.
I.Garrard & D.Streeter (1983) Macmillan London.

The Wild Flower Key.
F.Rose (2006) Frederick Warne.

The Wild Flowers of Britain and Europe.
R.Fitter, A.Fitter, M.Blamey (2003) A.& C.Black.

Complete Guide to British Wild Flowers.
Paul Sterry (2006) Harper Collins.

New Flora of the British Isles.
C.Stace (1997) Cambridge University Press.

North Yorkshire – Studies of its Botany, Geology, Climate and Physical Geography.
J.G.Baker (1906) Yorkshire Naturalists' Union.

B.S.B.I. Handbooks. Illustrated identification guides to groups and families of plants.
Botanical Society of the British Isles c/o British Museum (Natural History).

Wild Plants and their Habitats in the North York Moors.
(1993) Nan Sykes, North York Moors National Park.

Wild Flowers of the North Yorkshire Coast
(2004) Nan Sykes. North York Moors National Park.

INDEX

The author

Nan Sykes was born, and has lived most of her life, in
North East Yorkshire. As a rural journalist, a life-long interest
in natural history grew until early retirement enabled a full-time
commitment to the study of wildlife.

Focusing on wild flowers, she undertook botanical surveys
in Yorkshire and Cumbria, including a study of the
North Yorkshire coastal flora. She participated in a complete
survey of roadside verges and rail tracks throughout
North East Yorkshire and organised a scheme to map the
composition and distribution of botanical species throughout
the North York Moors National Park. The severe decline of
farmland flowers which this revealed led to her involvement in
the setting up at Ryedale Folk Museum of the
Cornfield Flowers conservation project and initiation of the
Sleights and North East Yorks Botanical Group.

Nan Sykes is a long-term member and formerly served
on the council of the YWT and its North-east Regional Group;
she is currently involved with local plant surveys
and conservation schemes.